THE ART OF CHORDS II
CHORD PROGRESSIONS - A COMPOSER'S GUIDE

Written by Stéphane Gagnon
Cover art by the author

Web site supported at
www.guitar-tracks.com

ISBN 0-9684809-6-9
Published by: Les éditions M.A.C.S. inc.
e mail: macs@guitar-tracks.com

Ut *queant laxis*
Resonare fibris
Mira gestorum
Famuli tuorum
Solve polluti
Labii reatum
Sancte **I**oannes

A hymn to St-John the Baptist

Introduction

Welcome to **THE ART OF CHORDS II**.

Did you ever wonder how some composers, whether contemporary or classical, could be so prolific? What techniques did a Mozart or Bach use to write one masterpiece after another? "Pure talent" will you say? Well, there must have been lots of it, but talent alone is not enough. Composers and songwriters from now and then are using a number of tools and bendable rules, one of which is called chord progressions. Basically, it means knowing what chord or scale degree to play next in a composition.

We are still using some of the same chord sequences used since J.S. Bach. It is fun to discover that a progression used by Frédéric Chopin (1810-1849), is the same one used by the Eagles in *Hotel California*. It sure gives a new meaning to *classic rock* doesn't it?

The introduction of jazz and modern music brought new rule-breaking concepts in chord resolutions and modes, greatly expanding the possibilities. The style of music you will achieve using the following chord tables and progressions is dependent on several factors: rhythm, sound, instrumentation, tempo, use of chord extensions and substitutions, use of scales... and add creativity to the list.

This volume is not guitar specific and is designed as a reference and workbook valid for all instruments. It is pre-supposed that you have some understanding of chord construction and notation on your instrument. Guitar players may want to check the first book of this series for full enjoyment.

Some recommendations:

- Read the table of contents so you don't miss anything.

- Have your instrument ready and play in all keys. Chord tables have been laid out for you so that transposing is an easy task.

- Detach the extra center page and try the chord progressions outlined with different modes and see what sounds good to you. Apply your own style!

- Write in the book, it's yours!

- Play, play, play and keep it fun!

Ready?

Table of contents

Using this book

Some of you will be surprised not to find any musical notation in the book. The truth is, it would have been too restrictive and taken too much space to illustrate all the options in standard notes. If you have a hard time with chord names, **take a look at page 46** before you begin. You will find a definition of most usable chords written in both standard and alternate chord notation. Both types are used in the book and are fairly easy to understand. The keyboard layout in the key of C shown at the bottom of that page will make it easy to find any chord. In the meantime, the following should help you understand where the different symbols apply (**X stands for: Any chord**).

Standard	X	♭9	sus2	m	M	sus4	♭5		#5	♭♭7	7	maj7	
Degree	1	♭2	2	♭3	3	4	♭5	5	#5	6	♭7	7	8
Alternate	X	♭9	9	-		11	#11		+	13	7	Δ	

Below is a typical table we will use in the book.

- You can see it as a **sequence of chords** with options displayed in the gray area, and basic chords (triads) transposed below in every key.

- You can also read chord names as **single notes from the given scale** in every key.

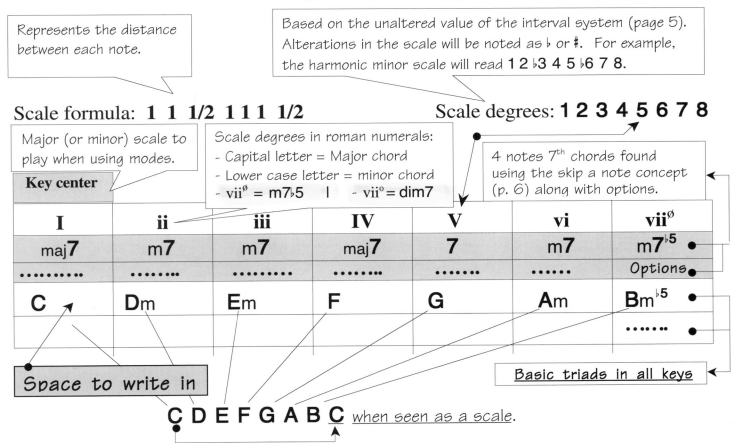

Represents the distance between each note.

Based on the unaltered value of the interval system (page 5). Alterations in the scale will be noted as ♭ or #. For example, the harmonic minor scale will read 1 2 ♭3 4 5 ♭6 7 8.

Scale formula: **1 1 1/2 1 1 1 1/2**   Scale degrees: **1 2 3 4 5 6 7 8**

Major (or minor) scale to play when using modes.

Key center

Scale degrees in roman numerals:
- Capital letter = Major chord
- Lower case letter = minor chord
- vii° = m7♭5 | - vii° = dim7

4 notes 7th chords found using the skip a note concept (p. 6) along with options.

I	ii	iii	IV	V	vi	vii°
maj7	m7	m7	maj7	7	m7	m7♭5
....	....	....	....	....	....	Options
C	Dm	Em	F	G	Am	Bm♭5
						....

Space to write in

Basic triads in all keys

C D E F G A B C when seen as a scale.

Use these tables with the chord sequences outlined in the book, or create your own progression. There is no specific rhythmic pattern here, and no need to play complete sequences. Take what you want from a progression. Repeat the first two chords for eight bars if you wish. Use them, as you need them. To keep things simple, play triads instead of 7th chords. What you see here are conventions (and proposals), not absolute rules. Feel free to experiment and go beyond. Oh yes! There is only one thing: Does it sound good to you?

The model of the major scale

The infamous scale we all learned as a child, the basic *Do Re Mi Fa Sol La Si Do*, is at the heart of how we think and calculate music. The names given to those notes come from a monk of the 11th century, Guido d'Arezzo, who discovered that using syllables to teach chants made it possible to learn new ones more quickly. He proposed that the first syllables of the first six phrases of the Latin text *a hymn to St. John the Baptist (see inside page)*, would be used to name music notes. The *Do,* originally *Ut,* was replaced for practical reasons. The *Si,* came later on in music literature. Prior to that, the letters *C D E F G A (B)*, which have been preserved in German languages, were the common names for notes.

The sequence of notes C D E F G A B C is divided by intervals of **tones** and **half tones** in the following way:

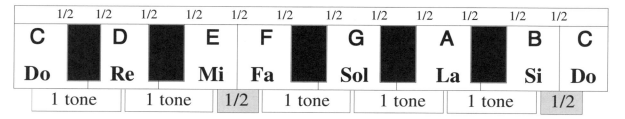

In occidental music, the 1/2 tone is the smallest distance between two notes. One tone is made out of two 1/2 tones.

The interval sequence **1 1 1/2 1 1 1 1/2** can be found in the *Ionian* mode of the *diatonic* major scale **in all keys** and will serve as a rule to measure and name any interval.

The *Ionian* mode is the first mode of the major scale, just like playing the present C scale. The word *"diatonic"*, means that each note of the scale will have a different name.

In opposition, scales displaying notes of the same name altered by a sharp or a flat (#, ♭), are said to be *chromatic*.

Here is the complete sequence of notes with their enharmonic equivalents.

	1/2	1/2	1/2	1/2	1/2	1/2	1/2	1/2	1/2	1/2	1/2	1/2
C	C#	D	D#	E	F	F#	G	G#	A	A#	B	C
	D♭		E♭	F♭	E#	G♭		A♭	B♭♭	B♭	C♭	B#

Repeat

By numbering the C scale from 1 to 8, we get:

Diatonic major scale of C - Ionian mode								
-Scale	C	D	E	F	G	A	B	C
-Interval	1	2	3	4	5	6	7	8
-Steps		1	1	1/2	1	1	1	1/2
-Name The tonic gives its name to the scale, the key and the chord.	TONIC	SECOND	THIRD	FOURTH	FIFTH	SIXTH	SEVENTH	OCTAVE

The spacing of the major scale defines the unaltered value of the interval system. Taking the root (or tonic) as a starting point, we get the following:

1 to **1** = **0**	tones = unison	
1 to **2** = **1**	tone = major second	
1 to **3** = **2**	tones = major third	
1 to **4** = **$2^{1/2}$**	tones = **perfect** fourth	
1 to **5** = **$3^{1/2}$**	tones = **perfect** fifth	
1 to **6** = **$4^{1/2}$**	tones = major sixth	
1 to **7** = **$5^{1/2}$**	tones = major seventh	
1 to **8** = **6**	tones = octave	

As a musician / composer, these values will be essential to your survival.

Why perfect, why major?   An interval is perfect when the two notes forming it are in each other's scale. If not (and unaltered), it is a major interval.

1 Tonic	**2** supertonic	**3** Mediant	**4** Sub-dominant
PERFECT	MAJOR	MAJOR	PERFECT
PERFECT	MAJOR	MAJOR	PERFECT
5 Dominant	**6** Superdominant	**7** Leading tone	**8** Octave

Altered intervals are named according to the following rules:

Any interval raised	**by a 1/2 tone**	**becomes augmented**
Perfect intervals reduced	**by a 1/2 tone**	**become diminished**
Major intervals reduced	**by a 1/2 tone**	**become minor**
Minor intervals reduced	**by a 1/2 tone**	**become diminished**

Interval	*notation*	*tone*		*example*
unison	**1**	**0**	tone	------ **C – C**
minor second	♭2	1/2	tone	------ C – D♭
major second	2	1	tone	------ C – D
minor third	**♭3**	**$1^{1/2}$**	**tone**	------ **C – E♭**
major third	**3**	**2**	**tones**	------ **C – E**
perfect fourth	4	$2^{1/2}$	tones	------ C – F
augmented fourth	♯4	3	tones	------ C – F♯
diminished fifth	♭5	3	tones	------ C – G♭
perfect fifth	**5**	**$3^{1/2}$**	**tones**	------ **C – G**
augmented fifth	♯5	4	tones	------ C – G♯
minor sixth	♭6	4	tones	------ C – A♭
major sixth	6	$4^{1/2}$	tones	------ C – A
minor seventh	7	5	tones	------ C – B♭
major seventh	maj7	$5^{1/2}$	tones	------ C – B
octave	**8**	**6**	**tones**	------ **C – C**
diminished ninth	♭9	$6^{1/2}$	tones	------ C – D♭
major ninth	9	7	tones	------ C – D
augmented ninth	♯9	$7^{1/2}$	tones	------ C – D♯
perfect eleventh	11	$8^{1/2}$	tones	------ C – F
augmented eleventh	♯11	9	tones	------ C – F♯
diminished thirteenth	♭13	10	tones	------ C – A♭
major thirteenth	13	$10^{1/2}$	tones	------ C – A

Chords formed by the major scale

The diatonic major scale gives birth to a specific set of chords created using only the notes from the scale. These *scale-tone-chords* are usually formed by super-imposing major and minor thirds.

That is basically **skipping one note out of two in the scale**.

For example, the C chord is created using three notes: C E G ⟶ $\overset{3}{\frown}$ $\overset{\flat3}{\frown}$ C D E F G A B

By using a major 3rd (2 tones) and a minor 3rd ($1^{1/2}$ tone), we get the following options:

> Major 3rd + minor 3rd = major chord
> Minor 3rd + major 3rd = minor chord
> Major 3rd + major 3rd = augmented chord
> Minor 3rd + minor 3rd = diminished chord

If we apply this method saying that every note of the C scale represents the root of a chord, we get a sequence of *three notes chords* (triads), which reads as follow:

C, Dm, Em, F, G, Am, Bdim.

These **triads** are only composed of notes included in the scale and could be found using the *skip a note* concept.

	Chord	Notes
I	C	C E G
ii	Dm	D F A
iii	Em	E G B
IV	F	F A C
V	G	G B D
vi	Am	A C E
vii°	Bdim	B D F

1	2	3	4	5	6	7	8
C	D	E	F	G	A	B	C
D	E	F	G	A	B	C	D
E	F	G	A	B	C	D	E
F	G	A	B	C	D	E	F
G	A	B	C	D	E	F	G
A	B	C	D	E	F	G	A
B	C	D	E	F	G	A	B

By adding another 3rd on top of the previous ones, we create a **four notes chord** called a **diatonic 7th chord**.

	Chord	Notes
I	Cmaj7	C E G B
ii	Dm7	D F A C
iii	Em7	E G B D
IV	Fmaj7	F A C E
V	G7	G B D F
vi	Am7	A C E G
vii^ø	Bm7$^{\flat5}$	B D F A

1	2	3	4	5	6	7	8
C	D	E	F	G	A	B	C
D	E	F	G	A	B	C	D
E	F	G	A	B	C	D	E
F	G	A	B	C	D	E	F
G	A	B	C	D	E	F	G
A	B	C	D	E	F	G	A
B	C	D	E	F	G	A	B

If you only play these chords in a given tonality, you'll sound good in a majority of styles.

In the context of this book, chords written as **maj7** can be played as major triads (**M**), chords written as **m7** can be played as minor triads (**m**). Alterations of the 5th should be respected, or the 5th eliminated ($X^{no\,5}$ or $Xm^{no\,5}$).

Other chords can be created by the major scale using a similar concept and a few variations.

Any major 3rd can be pushed to the 4th if it is a perfect 4th.

Chord	Notes
Csus4	C F G
Dm	D F A
Em	E G B
F	F A C
Gsus4	G C D
Am	A C E
Bdim	B D F

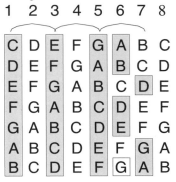

```
1 2 3 4 5 6 7 8
C D E F G A B C
D E F G A B C D
E F G A B C D E
F G A B C D E F
G A B C D E F G
A B C D E F G A
B C D E F G A B
```

With four note chords, the 7th or maj7 can be replaced by a major 6th.

Chord	Notes
C6	C E G B
Dm6	D F A C
Em7	E G B D
F6	F A C E
G6	G B D F
Am7	A C E G
Bm6♭5	B D F A

```
1 2 3 4 5 6 7 8
C D E F G A B C
D E F G A B C D
E F G A B C D E
F G A B C D E F
G A B C D E F G
A B C D E F G A
B C D E F G A B
```

Lowering **7** to **6** in this case creates an inversion of the G chord (G/B) and is therefore not useful. Actually, **Bm7♭5 = G9** without a root and serves a similar function. From a classical harmony stand point, **VIIm7♭5** is usually written **V9**.

This is how the *skip a note* looks when carried over to the 13th degree:

☐ = Avoid note

Avoid notes may be OK as passing notes but sound awkward in a chord structure because of their dissonant ♭9 relationship with one of the notes from the first octave. You may choose to use them to create tensions, or remove the incompatible note in the first octave.

Chord	Avoid	Notes
Cmaj13	11	C E G B D A
Dm11	13	D F A C G B
Em11	♭9, ♭13	E G B D A
Fmaj13	none	F A C E G B D
G13	3 with sus4	G B D F A C E
Am11	♭13	A C E G B D
Bm7♭5♭13	♭9	B D F A G

```
1  2  3  4  5  6  7  8  9  10 11 12 13
C  D  E  F  G  A  B  C  D  E  F  G  A
D  E  F  G  A  B  C  D  E  F  G  A  B
E  F  G  A  B  C  D  E  F  G  A  B  C
F  G  A  B  C  D  E  F  G  A  B  C  D
G  A  B  C  D  E  F  G  A  B  C  D  E
A  B  C  D  E  F  G  A  B  C  D  E  F
B  C  D  E  F  G  A  B  C  D  E  F  G
```

In the scale structure, **9 = 2 / 11 = 4 / 13 = 6**

You will find more options in the following tables but please feel free to experiment.

Scale degrees and Roman numeral notation

The different notes of a scale occupy a specific position called *degree* that is defined using *Roman numerals*. Keeping our example in the key of C, the note sequence C D E F G A B looks like this:

C	Dm	Em	F	G7	Am	Bm7$^{\flat 5}$
I	II	**III**	IV	V	**VI**	VII

The Roman numeral notation is used in chord progressions to define a sequence of chords to be played. It is valid for **any** major or minor scale, in **any** key. **Roman numerals will adopt the chord and note value prescribed by the scale**. In the harmonic minor scale (page 28), this is what we get:

Cm	Dm7$^{\flat 5}$	E$\flat$	Fm	G7	A$\flat$	Bdim
I	II	**III**	IV	V	**VI**	VII

The value of **degrees I to VII** in the above example is variable and depends on the scale. All it says is: play the chords formed on the (e.g.) 3rd and 6th degree of the scale.

To illustrate, here is the most common chord progression found in music: **I – IV – V – I**.

In C major, we have: Cmaj7, Fmaj7, G7, Cmaj7

I	IV	V	I

Same key, same degrees, different scales, different chords.

In C minor, we have: Cm, Fm7, G7, Cm

In the tables of this book, scale degrees written in capital letters are major – *e.g.:* **IV**, scale degrees written in lower case letters are minor – *e.g.:* **ii**, half diminished chords (or **m7**$^{\flat 5}$) are written – *e.g.:* **vii$^{\o}$**, diminished chords are written – *e.g.:* **vii^{o}**, augmented chords are written – *e.g.:* **V^{+}**.

Any symbol in parenthesis is optional.

This works well if you know which scale you are working with, but some chord progressions apply to many scale. They are written all in capitals like in the above example.

Since chords are formed by scales, we can say that **for the purpose of chord progressions, chord = scale = arpeggio = any trick of the trade you may use in a given key.**

It is important to note that within the major scale;

I and **IV** are <u>maj7</u>

V is the <u>only</u> dominant **7** chord

II, III and **VI** are **m7**

VII is the <u>only</u> **m7**$^{\flat 5}$

This observation is most useful in finding the tonality of a diatonic major progression.

Finding the key

In chord progressions or fake book type chord sequences, the key you are playing in may not always be clear. Diatonic major songs and musical compositions do not always start from the root chord but leave behind a set of clues we will use.

If you look at the previous page, you will see that the dominant 7 chord only appears on the **V** position in the sequence. Find the V^7 chord and you can deduct the root. It is located $3^{1/2}$ tones below **V**. Here is an example:

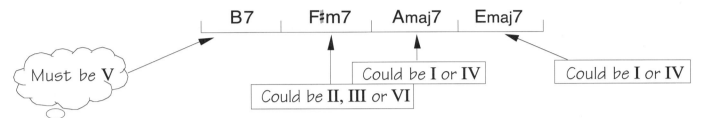

B7 being V^7, the note located $3^{1/2}$ steps below is E: the tonality is **E major**
The chord progression is: **V – II – IV – I**

The V^7 chord may not be present in the sequence. You could look for the **maj7** chord instead. It only falls on **I** and **IV**. You will need to compare it to the m7 chords.

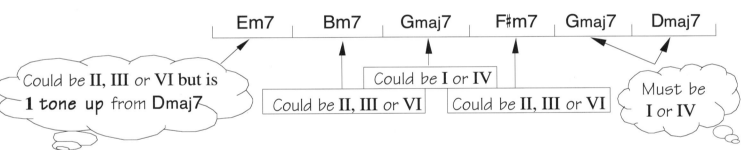

So, is the root chord Dmaj7 or Gmaj7? It is Dmaj7 and here is why:
In the major scale chord sequence, **I** is followed by **IIm7** --------- **IV** is followed by V^7.
If you find an Xm7 chord one tone up from an Xmaj7, that Xmaj7 is the root chord.
The chord progression is: **II – VI – IV – III – IV – I**.

The sequence may not have any 7th chords at all, as is often the case in pop music.

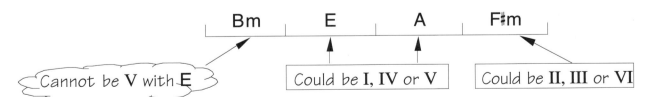

The notes B, E, A and F# are all included in both E and A scales. The clue here is that **B** is **V** to **E** and cannot be minor. The key is **A**. At a point, it all comes down to logic. **The chord progression is**: **II – V – I – VI**.

Progressions and chord stability

We can define three distinct groups of chords within the major scale built around the central chords **I, IV and V**. These groups are function of the stability of each chord. In general, compositions will build up from *stable* to *unstable* then back to a *stable chord*. You'll want to create a tension resolved by a stable chord, hence the **I – IV – V – I** progression in its simplest form.

Here is how it works: Notes are taken from the 1 2 3 4 5 6 7 8 scale formula

Group	Function	Chord	Notes			Originality
I Tonic group	Stable **I** *Starts well, ends well.* **VI** *cannot end a piece.*	I iii vi	1 3 6	3 5 1	5 7 3	Always contains **3**, never contains **4** **vi** is relative minor of **I**
IV Sub dominant group	Semi-stable *4 wants to go back to 3*	IV ii	4 2	6 4	1 6	Always contains **4** (and **6**) **ii** is relative minor of **IV**
V Dominant group	Unstable *7 wants to go up to 8* *2 wants to go back to 1*	V vii°	5 7	7 2	2 4	Always contains **2** and **7** **4** is the 7th of **5** **vii**° is a shortened **V**^{9} chord

Using chord functionality, **I – IV – V** can be replaced by **I - III – IV – II – V** or **I – VI – II – VII – I** ...

Here are some simple chord progressions. Use them in conjunction with the table on the right page. Try out several tonalities and merge one progression with another; experiment! Change some of the chords using chord functionality. Alternate endings are provided for progressions 7 to 12.

			Endings
1- **I – IV – V – I**	7- **II – V – I – IV – VII**		**IV – V – I**
2- **I – II – V – I**	8- **I – III – VI – IV –**		**II – V – I**
3- **I – II – IV – V – I**	9- **I – VII – I – VI – IV – I –**		**II – IV – I**
4- **I – IV – II – V – I**	10- **I – III – IV – VII – III – VI –**		**V – IV – I**
5- **I – III – IV – II – V – I**	11- **I – V – II – VI – IV – VII –**		**II – IV – V – I**
6- **I – V – I – IV – I – V – I**	12- **I – IV – VII – III – VI –**		**II – V – IV – I**

On fretted instruments, find these progressions in closed positions (barred chords) so they can be transposed easily. To keep it simple, play triads instead of 7th chords (page 6).

These progressions can be seen in two different ways.

1- As a simple chord on chord sequence: (e.g.: 1-) | D | G | A7 | D |

2- As anything you can play on a specific degree: (e.g.: 4-)

C	Cmaj7	C^{sus4}	C^{add9}	Fmaj7	F6	F	F$^{\flat5\ add13}$
I				**IV**			

Dm	Dm6	Dm7	Dm	G7	G7^{sus4}	G6	G7 :‖
II				**V**			

The Ionian major scale

See center page for more

The Ionian mode is the first mode of the major scale (known as major scale) and serves as a basis for six additional modes. **It is the most common and widely used scale in music.**

Scale formula: **1 1 1/2 1 1 1 1/2**   Scale degrees: **1 2 3 4 5 6 7 8**

Key center

I	ii	iii	IV	V	vi	vii°
maj7	m7	m7	maj7	7	m7	m7♭5
maj9	m9/11	m7add11	maj9	9/11/13	m9	
6, 6/9	m6		6/9	sus4	m11	
sus4	m6/9		♭5add13	Q(3)		
C	Dm	Em	F	G	Am	Bm♭5
D♭	E♭m	Fm	G♭	A♭	B♭m	Cm♭5
D	Em	F#m	G	A	Bm	C#m♭5
E♭	Fm	Gm	A♭	B♭	Cm	Dm♭5
E	F#m	G#m	A	B	C#m	D#m♭5
F	Gm	Am	B♭	C	Dm	Em♭5
G♭	A♭m	B♭m	C♭	D♭	E♭m	Fm♭5
G	Am	Bm	C	D	Em	F#m♭5
A♭	B♭m	Cm	D♭	E♭	Fm	Gm♭5
A	Bm	C#m	D	E	F#m	G#m♭5
B♭	Cm	Dm	E♭	F	Gm	Am♭5
B	C#m	D#m	E	F#	G#m	A#m♭5

- Write down two variations of the following progressions in Ionian mode:

Key of **E**: **I, IV, V, I**

Key of **A**: **I, II, V, I**

-Find the key and the key center for these progressions. Write them down numerically.

/ E9 / Amaj7 / Dmaj7 / E7 / Amaj7 /

/ Fmaj7 / B♭maj7 / Am7 / C7 / Fmaj7 /

Key   Center   Numerical

The modes of the major scale

Using modes is not as complicated as it may sound. Actually, we've already touched the subject when looking for chord types on pages 6 and 7.

Modes of the major scale (or any other) are created thinking of every note of the scale, as the tonic of another scale containing all the same notes, and applied when playing a given degree.

They can also be interpreted as a brand new chord system where diatonic 7th chords fall differently on each degree of the scale. Playing a I - IV - V – I doesn't sound the same in major or in the Aeolian mode.

Including the Ionian major scale itself (e.g. in **C**), we could create 7 different modes.

Modes	Notes	Scale formula
Ionian mode	C D E F G A B C	1 1 1/2 1 1 1 1/2
Dorian mode	D E F G A B C D	1 1/2 1 1 1 1/2 1
Phrygian mode	E F G A B C D E	1/2 1 1 1 1/2 1 1
Lydian mode	F G A B C D E F	1 1 1 1/2 1 1 1/2
Mixolydian	G A B C D E F G	1 1 1/2 1 1 1/2 1
Aeolian	A B C D E F G A	1 1/2 1 1 1/2 1 1
Locrian	B C D E F G A B	1/2 1 1 1/2 1 1 1

If you take a look at the scale formulas, you'll note that we are only moving the first interval to the end of the sequence as we go down the modes. This obviously changes note values within the scale but here are a few tricks:

> If the two first numbers add up to **2, the 3rd is major**,
> if the two first numbers add up to **$1^{1/2}$, the 3rd is minor**.
>
> If the last number is **1/2, the 7th is major**,
> if the last number is **1, the 7th is minor**.
>
> If the two last numbers add up to **2, the 6th is minor**,
> if the two last numbers add up to **$1^{1/2}$, the 6th is major**.

  Most used

Ionian	1	2	3	4	5	6	7	8	2	3	4	5	6	7
Dorian		1	2	♭3	4	5	6	♭7	8					
Phrygian			1	♭2	♭3	4	5	♭6	♭7	8				
Lydian				1	2	3	#4	5	6	7	8			
Mixolydian					1	2	3	4	5	6	♭7	8		
Aeolian						1	2	♭3	4	5	♭6	♭7	8	
Locrian							1	♭2	♭3	4	♭5	♭6	♭7	8

The Dorian mode

The Dorian mode is the second mode of the major scale and is widely used in Latin music.

Scale formula: **1 1/2 1 1 1 1/2 1**   Scale degrees: **1 2 ♭3 4 5 6 ♭7 8**

						Key center
i	**ii**	**III**	**IV**	**v**	**vi**$^{\varnothing}$	**VII**
m7	**m7**	**maj7**	**7**	**m7**	**m7♭5**	**maj7**
m9/11	m7^{add11}	maj9	9/11/13	m9		maj9
m6		6	sus4	m11		6, 6/9
m6/9		6/9	Q(3)			sus4
Dm	Em	F	G	Am	Bm$^{♭5}$	C
E♭m	Fm	G♭	A♭	B♭m	Cm$^{♭5}$	D♭
Em	F#m	G	A	Bm	C#m$^{♭5}$	D
Fm	Gm	A♭	B♭	Cm	Dm$^{♭5}$	E♭
F#m	G#m	A	B	C#m	D#m$^{♭5}$	E
Gm	Am	B♭	C	Dm	Em$^{♭5}$	F
A♭m	B♭m	C♭	D♭	E♭m	Fm$^{♭5}$	G♭
Am	Bm	C	D	Em	F#m$^{♭5}$	G
B♭m	Cm	D♭	E♭	Fm	Gm$^{♭5}$	A♭
Bm	C#m	D	E	F#m	G#m$^{♭5}$	A
Cm	Dm	E♭	F	Gm	Am$^{♭5}$	B♭
C#m	D#m	E	F#	G#m	A#m$^{♭5}$	B

-Write down two variations of the following progressions in Dorian mode:

Key of **D**: **I, IV, V, I**

Key of **B**: **I, II, V, I**

-Find the key and the key center for these progressions. Write them down numerically.

/ Em7 / F#m7 / Bm   / A /

/ C#m / Bmaj7 / F#7 / G#m /

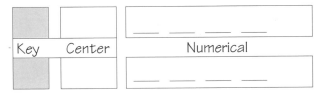

Key   Center   Numerical

The Phrygian mode

The Phrygian mode is the third mode of the major scale. Try a **I – II – I** sequence.

Scale formula: **1/2 1 1 1 1/2 1 1**   Scale degrees: **1 ♭2 ♭3 4 5 ♭6 ♭7 8**

					Key center	
i	**II**	**III**	**iv**	**V°**	**VI**	**vii**
m7	**maj7**	**7**	**m7**	**m7♭5**	**maj7**	**m7**
m7^{add11}	maj9 6 6/9	9/11/13 sus4 Q(♭3)	m9 m11		maj9 6, 6/9 sus4	m9/11 m6 m6/9
Em	F	G	Am	Bm♭5	C	Dm
Fm	G♭	A♭	B♭m	Cm♭5	D♭	E♭m
F#m	G	A	Bm	C#m♭5	D	Em
Gm	A♭	B♭	Cm	Dm♭5	E♭	Fm
G#m	A	B	C#m	D#m♭5	E	F#m
Am	B♭	C	Dm	Em♭5	F	Gm
B♭m	C♭	D♭	E♭m	Fm♭5	G♭	A♭m
Bm	C	D	Em	F#m♭5	G	Am
Cm	D♭	E♭	Fm	Gm♭5	A♭	B♭m
C#m	D	E	F#m	G#m♭5	A	Bm
Dm	E♭	F	Gm	Am♭5	B♭	Cm
D#m	E	F#	G#m	A#m♭5	B	C#m

-Write down two variations of the following progressions in Phrygian mode:

Key of **E**: **I, IV, II, III**

Key of **G**: **I, II, III, IV**

-Find the key and the key center for these progressions. Write them down numerically.

/ Em7 / Bm7$^{♭5}$ / G / Dm7 /

/ Cm7 / D♭ / E♭7 / Fm /

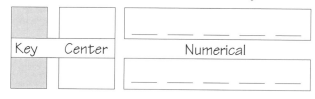

Key   Center   Numerical

The Lydian mode

The Lydian mode is the fourth mode of the major scale. Very close to its origins, it is found in many styles. It could be used as a "fake" *homonym* for the major scale (page 23).

Scale formula: **1 1 1 1/2 1 1 1/2**   Scale degrees: **1 2 3 ♯4 5 6 7 8**

				Key center		
I	**II**	**iii**	**iv°**	**V**	**vi**	**vii**
maj7	7	m7	m7♭5	maj7	m7	m7
maj9 6 6/9	9/11/13 sus4 Q(3)	m9 m11		maj9 6, 6/9 sus4	m9/11 m6 m6/9	m7add11
F	G	Am	Bm♭5	C	Dm	Em
G♭	A♭	B♭m	Cm♭5	D♭	E♭m	Fm
G	A	Bm	C♯m♭5	D	Em	F♯m
A♭	B♭	Cm	Dm♭5	E♭	Fm	Gm
A	B	C♯m	D♯m♭5	E	F♯m	G♯m
B♭	C	Dm	Em♭5	F	Gm	Am
C♭	D♭	E♭m	Fm♭5	G♭	A♭m	B♭m
C	D	Em	F♯m♭5	G	Am	Bm
D♭	E♭	Fm	Gm♭5	A♭	B♭m	Cm
D	E	F♯m	G♯m♭5	A	Bm	C♯m
E♭	F	Gm	Am♭5	B♭	Cm	Dm
E	F♯	G♯m	A♯m♭5	B	C♯m	D♯m

-Write down two variations of the following progressions in Lydian mode:

Key of **C**: **I, IV, V, I**

Key of **F**: **I, II, V, I**

-Find the key and the key center for these progressions. Write them down numerically.

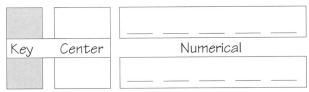

/ Fmaj7 / Cmaj7 / Em / Bm7♭5 / Fmaj7 /

/ D / C♯m / F♯m7 / A /

Key   Center   Numerical

The Mixolydian mode

The Mixolydian mode is the fifth mode of the major scale. One of its characteristics is the major chord build on the **VII** degree allowing the: **I – VII – IV – I** progression extensively used in pop and rock music. The **V** chord is minor but often replaced by a dominant 7th chord to preserve the **V – I** tension.

Scale formula: **1 1 1/2 1 1 1/2 1**   Scale degrees: **1 2 3 4 5 6 ♭7 8**

			Key center			
I	**ii**	**iii°**	**IV**	**v**	**vi**	**VII**
7	**m7**	**m7♭5**	**maj7**	**m7**	**m7**	**maj7**
9/11/13	m9		maj9	m9/11	m7add11	maj9
sus4	m11		6, 6/9	m6		6
Q(3)			sus4	m6/9		6/9
G	Am	Bm♭5	C	Dm	Em	F
A♭	B♭m	Cm♭5	D♭	E♭m	Fm	G♭
A	Bm	C♯m♭5	D	Em	F♯m	G
B♭	Cm	Dm♭5	E♭	Fm	Gm	A♭
B	C♯m	D♯m♭5	E	F♯m	G♯m	A
C	Dm	Em♭5	F	Gm	Am	B♭
D♭	E♭m	Fm♭5	G♭	A♭m	B♭m	C♭
D	Em	F♯m♭5	G	Am	Bm	C
E♭	Fm	Gm♭5	A♭	B♭m	Cm	D♭
E	F♯m	G♯m♭5	A	Bm	C♯m	D
F	Gm	Am♭5	B♭	Cm	Dm	E♭
F♯	G♯m	A♯m♭5	B	C♯m	D♯m	E

-Write down two variations of the following progressions in Mixolydian mode:

Key of **D**: **I, VII, IV, I**

Key of **A**: **I, II, VII, IV**

-Find the key and the key center for these progressions. Write them down numerically.

/ **E** / **D** / **A** / **A**sus4 /

Key	Center	Numerical
		_ _ _ _

/ **G** / **F**add9 / **A**m7 / **C** /

		_ _ _ _

(Keep the **G** on top for this one)

The Aeolian mode
Also known as pure minor or ancient minor

The sixth mode of the major scale has been in use for centuries. It was the *"official"* minor scale of the church modes with its minor chords on degrees I, IV and V. The major triads build on the ♭6th and on the ♭7th of the scale, allow the **I – VII – VI** descent so common in pop music. Still at the core of today's minor music, the Aeolian mode is worth your attention.

Scale formula: **1 1/2 1 1 1/2 1 1**   Scale degrees: **1 2 ♭3 4 5 ♭6 ♭7 8**

		Key center				
i	**ii°**	**III**	**iv**	**v**	**VI**	**VII**
m7	**m7♭5**	**maj7**	**m7**	**m7**	**maj7**	**7**
m9		maj9	m9/11	m7add11	maj9	9/11/13
m11		6, 6/9	m6		6	sus4
		sus4	m6/9		6/9	Q(3)
Am	Bm♭5	C	Dm	Em	F	G
B♭m	Cm♭5	D♭	E♭m	Fm	G♭	A♭
Bm	C♯m♭5	D	Em	F♯m	G	A
Cm	Dm♭5	E♭	Fm	Gm	A♭	B♭
C♯m	D♯m♭5	E	F♯m	G♯m	A	B
Dm	Em♭5	F	Gm	Am	B♭	C
E♭m	Fm♭5	G♭	A♭m	B♭m	C♭	D♭
Em	F♯m♭5	G	Am	Bm	C	D
Fm	Gm♭5	A♭	B♭m	Cm	D♭	E♭
F♯m	G♯m♭5	A	Bm	C♯m	D	E
Gm	Am♭5	B♭	Cm	Dm	E♭	F
G♯m	A♯m♭5	B	C♯m	D♯m	E	F♯

-Write down two variations of the following progressions in Aeolian mode:

Key of **F**: **I, IV, III, V**

Key of **A**: **I, III, VII, VI**

-Find the key and the key center for these progressions. Write them down numerically.

/ E♭m / B♭m / D♭7 / B7 /

/ Gm / F / E♭ / B♭ /

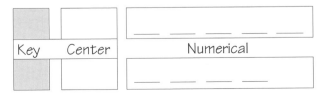

Key	Center		Numerical
			__ __ __ __
			__ __ __ __

II —————————— 17 ——————————

The Locrian mode

The Locrian mode is the seventh mode of the major scale. Not as much in use as the other modes, you will sometimes find it in Jazz.

Scale formula: 1/2 1 1 1/2 1 1 1   Scale degrees: 1 ♭2 ♭3 4 ♭5 ♭6 ♭7 8

	Key center					
i°	II	iii	iv	V	VI	vii
m7♭5	maj7	m7	m7	maj7	7	m7
	maj9, sus4	m6/9/11	m7add11	maj9, 6/9	9/11/13	m9/11
Bm♭5	C	Dm	Em	F	G	Am
C#m♭5	D	Em	F#m	G	A	Bm
D#m♭5	E	F#m	G#m	A	B	C#m
Em♭5	F	Gm	Am	B♭	C	Dm
F#m♭5	G	Am	Bm	C	D	Em
G#m♭5	A	Bm	C#m	D	E	F#m
A#m♭5	B	C#m	D#m	E	F#	G#m

The Harmonic major scale

Outside the modes created by the major scale, here is another mode-generating diatonic major scale. The harmonic major is an Ionian major scale with a ♭6.

Scale formula: 1 1 1/2 1 1/2 1½ 1/2   Scale degrees: 1 2 3 4 5 ♭6 7 8

Key center						
I	ii°	iii	iv	V	VI+	vii°
maj7	m7♭5	m7	mmaj7	7	maj7#5	dim7
Δ+, Δsus2/4, ♭13	dim9	7, 7+, /♭#9♭13 or	-6, °7, Δ°	6, 7sus4, ♭9/11/13	aug, ♭5, -Δ+	
C	D	E	F	G	A♭	B

	1	2	3	4	5	♭6	7	8	2	3	4	5	♭6	7
H.Major	1	2	3	4	5	♭6	7	8	2	3	4	5	♭6	7
Dorian ♭5		1	2	♭3	4	♭5	6	♭7	8					
Phrygian ♭4			1	♭2	♭3	♭4	5	♭6	♭7	8				
Lydian ♭3				1	2	♭3	#4	5	6	7	8			
Mixolydian ♭2					1	♭2	3	4	5	6	♭7	8		
Lydian #5, #2						1	#2	3	#4	#5	6	7	8	
Locrian ♭♭7							1	♭2	♭3	4	♭5	♭6	♭♭7	8

Adding to the puzzle

Here are a number of chords you could add to expand the tonal system of the major and harmonic minor scales (p.28). There is no real set of rules here, only some conventions and suggestions. Some of these concepts are applicable to other scales as well. All you need to do is calculate the distance between the relevant notes and apply the chord using the followings:

1- Secondary dominant chords and temporary tonics

Secondary dominants chords are located a 5th above another chord ($3^{1/2}$ tones up in major and harmonic minor scales). They have a function of: $V_{of}x$ (fifth of another chord).

Using secondary dominants is like making a parenthesis in a progression to create a relationship otherwise inexistent in the scale. You will usually find these new *out of scale* chords, right before or after the chord they relate to. In turn, the latter one takes a value of temporary tonic. This is equivalent to playing a **V – I** or a **I –V** in another key before coming back to the original tonality as it creates a mini *"tension – resolve"* passage within a progression.

Secondary dominant chords adopt the same characteristics as the **V** chord of the scale (V_{of} **I**). Within both major and harmonic minor scales, the **V** chord is an **X7** chord resolving perfectly on the temporary "**I**" it relates to.

In the major scale, secondary dominant chords ranging from **degrees II to VI** have a root that can be found in the scale. On the other hand, in both major and harmonic minor scales, V_{of} **VII** takes root on ♯**IV**, a dissonant tritone up from the root, and is not common.

Major scale						
V_{of}	**II**	**III**	**IV**	**V**	**VI**	**VII**
Same root as	**VI**	**VII**	**I**	**II**	**III**	♯**IV**
Play	VI^7	VII^7	I^7	II^7	III^7	♯IV^7
If in **C**	A7	B7	C7	D7	E7	F♯7

Harmonic minor scale						
V_{of}	**II**	**III**	**IV**	**V**	**VI**	**VII**
Same root as	♯**VI**	♭**VII**	**I**	**II**	**III**	♯**IV**
Play	♯VI^7	♭VII^7	I^7	II^7	III^7	♯IV^7
If in **Cm**	A7	B♭7	C7	D7	E♭7	F♯7

Try this progression in any key.

	V	**I**	V_{of} **VI**	**VI**	V_{of} **IV**	**IV**	V_{of} **II**	**II**	**V**	**I**
If in C:	G7	C	E7	Am	C7	F	A7	Dm	G7	C
If in Cm:	G7	Cm	E♭7	A♭	C7	Fm	A7	Dm$^{(♭5)}$	G	Cm

The 7th of $V_{of}x$ must go down to resolve on the 3rd of its parent chord; 1/2 a tone if the temporary tonic is major, 1 tone if it is minor.

Too many secondary chords can make you loose sight of the key. Still, here is an exercise:

I	V_{of} **II**	**II**	V_{of} **III**	**III**	V_{of} **IV**	**IV**	V_{of} **V**	**V**	V_{of} **VI**	**VI**	V_{of} **VII**	**VII**	**I**
											Uncommon		

Find the appropriate chords in both major and minor modes. Just remember that $V_{of}x$ is always located $3^{1/2}$ tones above *x* in scales where the 5th is perfect (see page 5).

2- Secondary leading tone chords

Secondary leading tone chords are played a 1/2 tone below the chord they relate to and create a tension very similar in function to the secondary dominant chords. Remember that the $m7^{\flat 5}$ chord created on the **VII**[th] degree of the major scale is equivalent to a V^9 without a root.

They work in the same location within a progression as the secondary dominants do and are placed before or after their related chord. This is equivalent to playing a **VII – I** or a **I – VII** in another key before coming back to the original tonality.

The **VII**[th] degree of the major scale is an **Xm7$^{\flat 5}$** chord and so is *VIIof x* in major, although often played as a **dim7** chord. It will appear as a **dim7** chord in the Harmonic minor scale, or as a dominant 7th chord placed one tone below in the Aeolian mode.

Major scale						
VIIof	**II**	**III**	**IV**	**V**	**VI**	**VII**
Same root as	$\flat$**II**	$\flat$**III**	**III**	$\flat$**V**	$\flat$**VI**	$\flat$**VII**
Play	$\flat$**II**m7$^{\flat 5}$	$\flat$**III**m7$^{\flat 5}$	**III**m7$^{\flat 5}$	$\flat$**V**m7$^{\flat 5}$	$\flat$**VI**m7$^{\flat 5}$	$\flat$**VII**m7$^{\flat 5}$
If in C	D$\flat$m7$^{\flat 5}$	E$\flat$m7$^{\flat 5}$	Em7$^{\flat 5}$	G$\flat$m7$^{\flat 5}$	A$\flat$m7$^{\flat 5}$	B$\flat$m7$^{\flat 5}$

Harmonic minor scale						
VIIof	**II**	**III**	**IV**	**V**	**VI**	**VII**
Same root as	$\flat$**II**	$\flat$**III**	$\flat$**IV**	$\flat$**V**	$\flat$**VI**	$\flat$**VII**
Play	$\flat$**II**dim	$\flat$**III**dim	$\flat$**IV**dim	$\flat$**V**dim	$\flat$**VI**dim	$\flat$**VII**dim
If in Cm	D$\flat$dim	Ddim	Edim	G$\flat$dim	Gdim	B$\flat$dim

Try this progression in any key.

	V	**I**	**_VIIof_ VI**	**VI**	**_VIIof_ IV**	**IV**	**_VIIof_ II**	**II**	**_Vof_ V** (Optional)	**V**	**I**
If in C:	G7	C	A$\flat$m7$^{\flat 5}$	Am	Em7$^{\flat 5}$	F	D$\flat$m7$^{\flat 5}$	Dm	D7	G7	C
If in Cm:	G7	Cm	Gdim	A$\flat$	Edim	Fm	D$\flat$dim	Dm7^{no5}	D7	G7	Cm

Too many secondary chords will make you loose sight of the key. Still, here is an exercise:

I	**_VIIof_ II**	**II**	**_Vof_ III**	**III**	**_Vof_ IV**	**IV**	**_VIIof_ V**	**V**	**_VIIof_ VI**	**VI**	**_VIIof_ VII**	**VII**	**I**

This one belongs to the domain of jazz exploration

The sequence *VIIof* **II** – **II** works better with the harmonic minor if **II** is played **m7**$^{no\ 5}$.

Find the appropriate chords in both major and minor modes.

3- Secondary sub-dominant chords

Secondary sub-dominant chords are formed a 5th below the chord on which they apply. Reaching $3^{1/2}$ tones below a note is equivalent to playing its 4th. This creates a much softer tension than the one we get with the secondary dominant or leading tone chords.

They work in the same location within a progression as the above mentioned do, and are mostly placed before or after a related chord. This is equivalent to playing a **IV – I** or a **I – IV** in another key before coming back to the original tonality.

The IVth degree of the major scale being an Xmaj7 chord, *IV*of *x* could be played as such in major mode, **or simply left as a basic triad** (1 3 5 as is often found in classical music). It will take the form of an Xm7 chord (or a 1♭3 5 triad) in minor mode, just like the IVth degree of the harmonic minor scale.

*IV*of **V** in major mode gives **I**maj7, which is already included in the scale.

Major scale						
***IV**of*	**II**	**III**	**IV**	**V**	**VI**	**VII**
Same root as	**V**	**VI**	**♭VII**	**I**	**II**	**III**
Play	**V**maj^7	**VI**maj^7	**♭VII**maj^7	**I**maj^7	**II**maj^7	**III**maj^7
If in **C**	Gmaj7	Amaj7	B♭maj7	Cmaj7	Dmaj7	Emaj7

Harmonic minor scale						
***IV**of*	**II**	**III**	**IV**	**V**	**VI**	**VII**
Same root as	**V**	**VI**	**♭VII**	**I**	**♭II**	**III**
Play	**V**m^7	**VI**m^7	**♭VII**m^7	**I**m^7	**♭II**m^7	**III**m^7
If in **Cm**	Gm7	A♭m7	B♭m7	Cm7	D♭m7	E♭m7

Try this: **I** – *IV*of **III** – **III** – *IV*of **IV** – **IV** – **I**   in both major and minor modes.

4- Secondary supertonic chords

In the same line of thought as the previous secondary chords, we could think of the ***II**of x* as a possible chord to add before or after a related chord. Here are the best options.

Major scale					Harmonic minor scale			
***II**of*	**I V**	**VI**	**VII**		***II**of*	**III**	**IV**	**VI**
Play	**V**m7	**VII**m7	**♭II**m7		**Play**	**IV**m7$^{♭5}$	**V**m7$^{♭5}$	**♭VII**m7$^{♭5}$

II ———————————— 21 ————————————

5- Creating a larger secondary parenthesis

It is possible to play several secondary chords before a given temporary tonic to prolong the tension period.

For example:

I	– II_{of} IV –	IV	–	II	– VI	–	VII_{of} V – V_{of} V	– V
Cmaj7	Gm7	Fmaj7	Dm7	Am7		F♯m7$^{♭5}$	D7	G$^{(7)}$

6- Half tone related chords

You could transform any chord of the scale by altering **one** of the notes **1**, **3**, **5** or **7** by a half tone (♯ or ♭). This will bend the rules with very interesting results.

7	m7	maj7	m^{maj7}	maj7$^{♯5}$	m7$^{♭5}$	dim7
Xm7	X7	X7	XΔ	XΔ	Xm7	X7$^{♭5}$
XΔ	X^{-}Δ	X^{-}Δ	X^{-}7	X7$^{♯5}$	X7$^{♭5}$	Xm7
X7$^{♯5}$	Xm^{6}	X^{+}Δ	X♭ aug	X♯$^{-}$7	X♭Δ	X♭7
X7$^{♭5}$	X^{-}7$^{♭5}$	X♯$^{-}$7$^{♭5}$				
X7^{sus4}	X♭Δ$^{♯5}$					
X♯^{o}7						

7- Extending chord progressions

Instead of playing chords one after the next, think of any progression (e.g.: I – IV – V) as "anything you could play on I", "anything you could play on IV" and so on. Here is an example with the I – IV –V:

| C | Cmaj7 | Cmaj7$^{♯5}$ | Cmaj9$^{♯5}$ | F | Fmaj7 | F6 | Fm6 | G | G7$^{♯5}$ | G7sus4 | G7 |

8- Tritone substitution

Mostly used in blues, the tritone substitution consist of replacing a dominant 7 chord by another dominant 7 chord located a ♭5 below. Although this concept could be applied to any dominant chord, it is widely used as a replacement for the V^{7}. Play a ♭II^{7} (D♭7 in C) chord instead of (or along with) a V^{7}. Try these out with the major scale:

I, IV, ♭II^{7}, V^{7}, I	I, IV, ♭II^{7}, I	IIm^{7}, ♭II^{7}, I	IIm^{7}, ♭II^{7}, V^{7}, I

Stretching it and thinking of an X7 chord on any degree of the scale, this is what we get.

Tritone of	I	II	III	IV	V	VI	VII
Play	♯IV^{7}	♯V^{7}	♭VII^{7}	VII^{7}	♭II^{7}	♭II^{7}	IV^{7}
	In used			In use	Widely used		

9- Altered Dominant chords

Another Blues concept is the use of altered dominant 7th chords to increase the already high tension of the X7 chords. Any dominant 7th chord can be altered regardless of its position. Just think of Jimmy Hendrix's "Purple Haze" starting with the high tension E7♯9 on the **I** chord. Alterations are done above the octave by adding the intervals of ♯9, ♭9, ♯11 or ♭13 to the X7 chord.

10- Homonym scales

Homonym scales simply bare the same key notes but have different modal notes (3 and 6). The scales of **C** and **Cm** are a good example of that. Chords formed on degrees I, III, IV and VI will be affected in this case. Chords can be *borrowed* from a homonym scale to create a modal ambiguity within a progression without changing the tonality. If you only borrow one (maybe two) chord from a homonym scale, it does not qualify as a complete modal change and is called **mixed mode**. Try: I C I Em I F I C I E♭ I F I **Fm** I C I G7sus4 I G I C I

Major mode: **I – IV – IVm – I**.   This one is a *gospel cadence*.

11- Augmented 6th chords

This is an idea coming straight from classical music and a bit too long to explain in detail. Here are the results of the calculations: In the possible of $x – V – I$: $x = $♭VI according to the unaltered value of the intervals found in the major scale; **A♭ in the key of C**. In the minor mode, the 6th is already altered with a flat but the location of the augmented sixth chord won't change, it will remain **A♭ in the key of Cm**.

We will find three different augmented sixth chords:

1- The French sixth (6thFr.)			Notation: $\frac{V}{of}$ V	4 notes chord			
Play: ♭VI$^{7\,\flat5}$			6th Fr.				
Examples:	Major scale	A♭$^{7\flat5}$ G^7 C			C$^{7\flat5}$ B^7 E		
	Minor scale	A♭$^{7\flat5}$ G^7 Cm			C$^{7\flat5}$ B^7 Em		

2- The Italian sixth (6th Ital.)			Notation: $\frac{V}{of}$ V	3 notes chord		
Play: ♭VI$^{7\,(no\,5)}$			6th Ital.			
Examples:	Major scale	G♭$^{7(no5)}$ F^7 B♭		D♭$^{7(no5)}$ C^7 F	
	Minor scale	G♭$^{7(no5)}$ F^7 B♭m		D♭$^{7(no5)}$ C^7 Fm	

3- The German sixth (6th Ger.)			Notation: $\frac{V}{of}$ V	4 notes chord		
Play: ♭VI^{7}			6th Ger.			
Examples:	Major scale	E♭^{7} D^7 G		D♭^{7} C^7 F	
	Minor scale	E♭^{7} D^7 Gm		D♭^{7} C^7 Fm	

The Neapolitan sixth *(N$_6$)*. This one fits in a different category, as it is not an augmented sixth chord but the first inversion of a major triad built on the ♭**II** of the scale (F, A♭, D♭ in the key of C and Cm).

Play: IVm$^{\sharp5}$	Note: *m♯5 does not exist as such but is a convenient way to indicate the first inversion of a major triad.*	Notation: N$_6$	3 notes chord		
Examples:	Major scale	Fm$^{\sharp5}$ G^7 C		Cm$^{\sharp5}$ D^7 G
	Minor scale	Fm$^{\sharp5}$ G^7 Cm		Cm$^{\sharp5}$ D^7 Gm

Building blocks for the I – IV – V

(A non-exhaustive List of) **Building blocks for the I – IV – V** (Be creative)
You may use several blocks in each group and repeat them as you please. Try different modes.

I	Link 1	IV	Link 2	V	I
I	None	IV	None	V	I
I – IV – I	VI	II	V_{of} V	V^7	VI
I – VII – I	II between I – IV	IV – II – IV	VII_{of} V	V – IV – V	
I – V – I	III between I – IV	II – I – II	I	V – I – V	
I – IV – VII	V	IV – II_{of} IV – IV	II	$\flat II^7$ Tritone subst	
I – VII – IV	IV_{of} IV	VII^7 Tritone subst·	III	$\flat II^7$ – II – V	
I – IV – II	V_{of} IV		III – IV		
I – IV – III	VII_{of} IV		IV (homonym)		
I – VI – I	VII_{of} VI – VI		VI		
I – VI –VII	V_{of} II – II		VII		
I – VII – VI	V_{of} III – III		N^6		
I – V – VI	VII_{of} III – III		6th Fr. Ital. Ger.		
I – III – VI	$\{$ II – VII_{of} III – III $\}$ – VII_{of} IV	*Optional* ← Go back to I ◆	$V^{Q(3)}$	*Optional* ← Go back to Link1, IV or link 2 ◆	

Harmonic marches

From classical... **Harmonic marches** ...to "classic" rock

1- I – IV – II –V – III – VI – II – V – I

2- I – V – II – VI –III –VII – IV – II – V – I

3- VI – II – I – IV – III – VI – V – I – II – V – I

4- I – V – VI – III – IV – I – II – VI – II – V – I ———— Pachelbel

5- I – V – I – III – V_{of} III – III – V – V_{of} V – V – I

6- I – V – I – VI – V_{of} VI – IV – V_{of} IV – II – V – I

7- V – I – V_{of} VI – VI – V_{of} IV – IV – V_{of} II – II – V – I ——— Handel

8- I – IV – II – V – III – VI – IV – VII –V – I – II –V – I ——— Beethoven

9- I – V – III – V_{of} III – V – V_{of} V – V – I – IV – II – V – I

10- I – V – I – II – V_{of} II – II – III – V_{of} III – III – IV – V – I

11- I – V – VII – V_{of} VII – VI – V_{of} VI – V – V_{of} V – IV – V_{of} VI – II – V – I — Chopin

Modulating marches

Modulating marches
You can stop and get out of modulating marches whenever you've reached a desired key (I = I).

12- II – V – I = II   Span 6 keys by descending tones

13- V_{of} V – V – I = V_{of} V

14- IV_{of} IV – IV – I = IV_{of} IV   Span 6 keys by ascending tones

15- IV – V – I = IV   Span 12 keys by ascending 5ths

16- $x – y – z – \mathbf{I} = \boldsymbol{x}$ / x, y and z can be a number of chords as long as x is different from **I**. (e.g.:) II – VI – IV – I = II…

Two events can occur when resolving the equation: $x – y – z – I = x$:

- **I and x are played with the same type** of diatonic 7th chord: For example, I and IV are both maj7 in the major scale and both minor triads in the harmonic minor scale. The resolve of I = x when x = IV or IV_{of}, creates no ambiguity (e.g.: 14, 15).

- **I and x are not of the same chord type**:
In this case, the equation I = x can be seen in two ways. Take n° 22 in major as an example and
play both I and I = II: | Dm7 | G7 | C | Cm7 | F7 | B♭ | B♭m7 | E♭7 | A♭ | A♭m7 |...

or play only I = II: | Dm7 | G7 | Cm7 | F7 | B♭m7 | E♭7 | A♭m7 | D♭7 | G♭m7 |...

The first method sounds like a series of step-by-step modulations, the second method is more fluid.

Diatonic major

Diatonic majo

Scal

I	ii	iii	I
maj7	m7	m7	ma
maj9	m9/11	m7add11	m
6/9	m6		6
sus4	m6/9		♭5a
C	Dm	Em	
D♭	E♭m	Fm	
D	Em	F#m	
E♭	Fm	Gm	
E	F#m	G#m	
F	Gm	Am	
G♭	A♭m	B♭m	
G	Am	Bm	
A♭	B♭m	Cm	
A	Bm	C#m	
B♭	Cm	Dm	
B	C#m	D#m	

Harmonic min

Scale

i	ii⌀	III(+)	i
m	m7♭5	M, aug	
mmaj7	dim7	maj7#5	m
		maj9#5	m7
m♭6		add9	dir
Cm	Dm♭5	E♭	F
C#m	D#m♭5	E	F#
Dm	Em♭5	F	G
E♭m	Fm♭5	G♭	A
Em	F#m♭5	G	A
Fm	Gm♭5	A♭	B
F#m	G#m♭5	A	B
Gm	Am♭5	B♭	C
A♭m	B♭m♭5	C♭	D
Am	Bm♭5	C	D
B♭m	Cm♭5	D♭	E
Bm	C#m♭5	D	E

THE ART OF CH

THE ART OF CHORDS II
CHORD PROGRESSIONS - A COMPOSER'S GUIDE

Double center page

Detach with care

Building blocks for the I – IV – V

(A non-exhaustive List of) **Building blocks for the I – IV – V** (Be creative)
You may use several blocks in each group and repeat them as you please. Try different modes.

I	Link 1	IV	Link 2	V	I
I	None	IV	None	V	I
I – IV – I	VI	II	V_{of} V	V^7	VI
I – VII – I	II between I – IV	IV – II – IV	VII_{of} V	V – IV – V	
I – V – I	III between I – IV	II – I – II	I	V – I – V	
I – IV – VII	V	IV – II_{of} IV – IV	II	$\flat II^7$ Tritone subst	
I – VII – IV	IV_{of} IV	VII^7 Tritone subst.	III	$\flat II^7$ – II – V	
I – IV – II	V_{of} IV		III – IV		
I – IV – III	VII_{of} IV		IV (homonym)		
I – VI – I	VII_{of} VI – VI		VI		
I – VI –VII	V_{of} II – II		VII		
I – VII – VI	V_{of} III – III		N^6		
I – V – VI	VII_{of} III – III	Optional	6th Fr. Ital. Ger.	Optional	
I – III – VI	{ II – VII_{of} III – III – VII_{of} IV }	← Go back to I ◆	$V^{Q(3)}$	← Go back to Link1, IV or link 2 ◆	

Harmonic marches

From classical... **Harmonic marches** ...to "classic" rock

1- I – IV – II –V – III – VI – II – V – I

2- I – V – II – VI –III –VII – IV – II – V – I

3- VI – II – I – IV – III – VI – V – I – II – V – I

4- I – V – VI – III – IV – I – II – VI – II – V – I ——————— Pachelbel

5- I – V – I – III – V_{of} III – III – V – V_{of} V – V – I

6- I – V – I – VI – V_{of} VI – IV – V_{of} IV – II – V – I

7- V – I – V_{of} VI – VI – V_{of} IV – IV – V_{of} II – II – V – I ——— Handel

8- I – IV – II – V – III – VI – IV – VII –V – I – II –V – I ——— Beethoven

9- I – V – III – V_{of} III – V – V_{of} V – V – I – IV – II – V – I

10- I – V – I – II – V_{of} II – II – III – V_{of} III – III – IV – V – I

11- I – V – VII – V_{of} VII – VI – V_{of} VI – V – V_{of} V – IV – V_{of} VI – II – V – I— Chopin

Modulating marches

Modulating marches
You can stop and get out of modulating marches whenever you've reached a desired key (I = I).

12- II – V – I = II — Span 6 keys by descending tones

13- V_{of} V – V – I = V_{of} V

14- IV_{of} IV – IV – I = IV_{of} IV — Span 6 keys by ascending tones

15- IV – V – I = IV — Span 12 keys by ascending 5^{ths}

16- $x - y - z - I = x$ / x, y and z can be a number of chords as long as x is different from I. (e.g.:) II – VI – IV – I = II...

Two events can occur when resolving the equation: $x - y - z - I = x$:

- **I and x are played with the same type** of diatonic 7th chord: For example, I and IV are both maj7 in the major scale and both minor triads in the harmonic minor scale. The resolve of I = x when x = IV or IV_{of}, creates no ambiguity (e.g.: 14, 15).

- **I and x are not of the same chord type**:
In this case, the equation I = x can be seen in two ways. Take n° 22 in major as an example and
play both I and I = II: | Dm7 | G7 | C | Cm7 | F7 | B♭ | B♭m7 | E♭7 | A♭ | A♭m7 |...

or **play only I = II**: | Dm7 | G7 | Cm7 | F7 | B♭m7| E♭7 | A♭m7 | D♭7 | G♭m7|...

The first method sounds like a series of step-by-step modulations, the second method is more fluid.

Diatonic major

Diatonic majo

Scal

I	ii	iii	IV
maj7	m^7	m^7	ma
maj9	$m^{9/11}$	m^7_{add11}	ma
$6^{/9}$	m^6		6
sus4	$m^{6/9}$		$\flat 5$
C	Dm	Em	
D♭	E♭m	Fm	
D	Em	F#m	
E♭	Fm	Gm	
E	F#m	G#m	
F	Gm	Am	
G♭	A♭m	B♭m	
G	Am	Bm	
A♭	B♭m	Cm	
A	Bm	C#m	
B♭	Cm	Dm	
B	C#m	D#m	

Harmonic min

Scale

i	ii$^{\emptyset}$	III$^{(+)}$	i
m	$m7^{\flat 5}$	M, aug	
m^{maj7}	dim7	$maj7^{\sharp 5}$	m6
		$maj9^{\sharp 5}$	m^7
$m^{\flat 6}$		add9	dim
Cm	$Dm^{\flat 5}$	E♭	Fr
C#m	$D\#m^{\flat 5}$	E	F#
Dm	$Em^{\flat 5}$	F	G
E♭m	$Fm^{\flat 5}$	G♭	A♭
Em	$F\#m^{\flat 5}$	G	Am
Fm	$Gm^{\flat 5}$	A♭	B♭
F#m	$G\#m^{\flat 5}$	A	B♭
Gm	$Am^{\flat 5}$	B♭	C♭
A♭m	$B\flat m^{\flat 5}$	C♭	D♭
Am	$Bm^{\flat 5}$	C	D♭
B♭m	$Cm^{\flat 5}$	D♭	E♭
Bm	$C\#m^{\flat 5}$	D	E

V of = 7, sus4, 7sus4   **VII of = m7♭5**   **IV of = maj7**   **II of = m7**   **Aug 6th**   **N6**

vi	vii°ø	II	III	IV	V	VI	VII	II	III	IV	V	VI	II	III	IV	VI	VII	IV	VI	VII	♭VI	IV
m7	m7♭5																				7	m#5
m9																					7♭5	
m11																					7 no5	
Am	Bm♭5	A	B	C	D	E	F#	D♭	E♭	E	G♭	A♭	G	A	B♭	D	E	G	B	C#	A♭	F
B♭m	Cm♭5	B♭	C	D♭	E♭	F	G	D	E	F	G	A	A♭	B♭	B	E♭	F	A♭	C	D	A	G♭
Bm	C#m♭5	B	C#	D	E	F#	G#	E♭	F	G♭	A♭	B♭	A	B	C	E	G♭	A	C#	D#	B♭	G
Cm	Dm♭5	C	D	E♭	F	G	A	E	F#	G	A	B	B♭	C	D♭	F	G	B♭	D	E	B	A♭
C#m	D#m♭5	C#	D#	E	F#	G#	A#	F	G	A♭	B♭	C	B	C#	D	F#	G#	B	D#	F	C	A
Dm	Em♭5	D	E	F	G	A	B	G♭	A♭	A	B	D♭	C	D	E♭	G	A	C	E	F#	D♭	B♭
E♭m	Fm♭5	E♭	F	G♭	A♭	B♭	C	G	A	B♭	C	D	D♭	E♭	E	A♭	B♭	C#	F	G	D	B
Em	F#m♭5	E	F#	G	A	B	C#	A♭	B♭	B	D♭	E♭	D	E	F	A	B	D	F#	G#	E♭	C
Fm	Gm♭5	F	G	A♭	B♭	C	D	A	B	C	D	E	E♭	F	G♭	B♭	C	D#	G	A	E	D♭
F#m	G#m♭5	F#	G#	A	B	C#	D#	B♭	C	D♭	E♭	F	E	F#	G	B	C#	E	G#	A#	F	D
Gm	Am♭5	G	A	B♭	C	D	E	B	D♭	D	E	G♭	F	G	A♭	C	D	F	A	B	G♭	E♭
G#m	A#m♭5	G#	A#	B	C#	D#	F	C	D	E♭	F	G	F#	G#	A	C#	D#	F#	A#	C	G	E

V of = 7, sus4, 7sus4   **VII of = dim7**   **IV of = m7**   **II of = m7♭5**   **Aug 6th**   **N6**

VI	vii°	II	III	IV	V	VI	VII	II	III	IV	V	VI	II	III	IV	VI	VII	III	IV	VI	♭VI	IV
maj7	dim7																				7	m#5
M	dim ♭5																				7♭5	
m(maj7) 6, m6	(#5)																				7 no5	
A♭	Bdim	A	B♭	C	D	E♭	F#	D♭	D	E	G♭	G	G	A♭	B♭	D♭	E	F	G	B♭	A♭	F
A	B#dim	B♭	B	D♭	E♭	E	G	D	E♭	F	G	A♭	A♭	A	B	D	F	G♭	A♭	B	A	G♭
B♭	C#dim	B	C	D	E	F	G#	E♭	E	G♭	A♭	A	A	B♭	C	E♭	G♭	G	A	C	B♭	G
C♭	Ddim	C	D♭	E♭	F	G♭	A	E	F	G	A	B♭	B♭	B	D♭	E	G	A♭	B♭	D♭	B	A♭
C	D#dim	C#	D	E	F#	G	A#	F	G♭	A♭	B♭	B	B	C	D	F	G#	A	B	D	C	A
D♭	Edim	D	E♭	F	G	A♭	B	G♭	G	A	B	C	C	D♭	E♭	G♭	A	B♭	C	E♭	D♭	B♭
D	E#dim	E♭	E	G♭	A♭	A	C	G	A♭	B♭	C	D♭	D♭	D	E	G	B♭	B	D♭	E	D	B
E♭	F#dim	E	F	G	A	B♭	C#	A♭	A	B	D♭	D	D	E♭	F	A♭	B	C	D	F	E♭	C
F♭	Gdim	F	G♭	A♭	B♭	B	D	A	B♭	C	D	E♭	E♭	E	G	A	C	C#	D#	F#	E	D♭
F	G#dim	F#	G	A	B	C	D#	B♭	B	D♭	E♭	E	E	F	G	B♭	C#	D	E	G	F	D
G♭	Adim	G	A♭	B♭	C	D♭	E	B	C	D	E	F	F	G♭	A♭	B	D	E♭	F	A♭	G♭	E♭
G	A#dim	G#	A	B	C#	D	F	C	D♭	E♭	F	G♭	F#	G	A	C	D#	E	F#	A	G	E

Double center page

Detach with care

ISBN 0-9684809-6-9
Published by: Les éditions M.A.C.S. inc.
e mail: macs@guitar-tracks.com
http://www.guitar-tracks.com

vi	viiø	V_{of} = 7, sus4, 7sus4						VII_{of} = m7♭5					IV_{of} = maj7					II_{of} = m7			Aug 6th	N6
		II	III	IV	V	VI	VII	II	III	IV	V	VI	II	III	IV	VI	VII	IV	VI	VII	♭VI	IV
m7	m7♭5																				7	m#5
m9																					7♭5	
m11																					7 no5	
Am	Bm♭5	A	B	C	D	E	F#	D♭	E♭	E	G♭	A♭	G	A	B♭	D	E	G	B	C#	A♭	F
B♭m	Cm♭5	B♭	C	D♭	E♭	F	G	D	E	F	G	A	A♭	B♭	B	E♭	F	A♭	C	D	A	G♭
Bm	C#m♭5	B	C#	D	E	F#	G#	E♭	F	G♭	A♭	B♭	A	B	C	E	G♭	A	C#	D#	B♭	G
Cm	Dm♭5	C	D	E♭	F	G	A	E	F#	G	A	B	B♭	C	D♭	F	G	B♭	D	E	B	A♭
C#m	D#m♭5	C#	D#	E	F#	G#	A#	F	G	A♭	B♭	C	B	C#	D	F#	G#	B	D#	F	C	A
Dm	Em♭5	D	E	F	G	A	B	G♭	A♭	A	B	D♭	C	D	E♭	G	A	C	E	F#	D♭	B♭
E♭m	Fm♭5	E♭	F	G♭	A♭	B♭	C	G	A	B♭	C	D	D♭	E♭	E	A♭	B♭	C#	F	G	D	B
Em	F#m♭5	E	F#	G	A	B	C#	A♭	B♭	B	D♭	E♭	D	E	F	A	B	D	F#	G#	E♭	C
Fm	Gm♭5	F	G	A♭	B♭	C	D	A	B	C	D	E	E♭	F	G♭	B♭	C	D#	G	A	E	D♭
F#m	G#m♭5	F#	G#	A	B	C#	D#	B♭	C	D♭	E♭	F	E	F#	G	B	C#	E	G#	A#	F	D
Gm	Am♭5	G	A	B♭	C	D	E	B	D♭	D	E	G♭	F	G	A♭	C	D	F	A	B	G♭	E♭
G#m	A#m♭5	G#	A#	B	C#	D#	F	C	D	E♭	F	G	F#	G#	A	C#	D#	F#	A#	C	G	E

VI	viio	V_{of} = 7, sus4, 7sus4						VII_{of} = dim7					IV_{of} = m7					II_{of} = m7♭5			Aug 6th	N6
		II	III	IV	V	VI	VII	II	III	IV	V	VI	II	III	IV	VI	VII	III	IV	VI	♭VI	IV
maj7	dim7																				7	m#5
M	dim																				7♭5	
m(maj7)	♭5																				7 no5	
6, m6	(#5)																					
A♭	Bdim	A	B♭	C	D	E♭	F#	D♭	D	E	G♭	G	G	A♭	B♭	D♭	E	F	G	B♭	A♭	F
A	B#dim	B♭	B	D♭	E♭	E	G	D	E♭	F	G	A♭	A♭	A	B	D	F	G♭	A♭	B	A	G♭
B♭	C#dim	B	C	D	E	F	G#	E♭	E	G♭	A♭	A	A	B♭	C	E♭	G♭	G	A	C	B♭	G
C♭	Ddim	C	D♭	E♭	F	G♭	A	E	F	G	A	B♭	B♭	B	D♭	E	G	A♭	B♭	D♭	B	A♭
C	D#dim	C#	D	E	F#	G	A#	F	G♭	A♭	B♭	B	B	C	D	F	G#	A	B	D	C	A
D♭	Edim	D	E♭	F	G	A♭	B	G♭	G	A	B	C	C	D♭	E♭	G♭	A	B♭	C	E♭	D♭	B♭
D	E#dim	E♭	E	G♭	A♭	A	C	G	A♭	B♭	C	D♭	D♭	D	E	G	B♭	B	D♭	E	D	B
E♭	F#dim	E	F	G	A	B♭	C#	A♭	A	B	D♭	D	D	E♭	F	A♭	B	C	D	F	E♭	C
F♭	Gdim	F	G♭	A♭	B♭	B	D	A	B♭	C	D	E♭	E♭	E	G♭	A	C	C#	D#	F#	E	D♭
F	G#dim	F#	G	A	B	C	D#	B♭	B	D♭	E♭	E	E	F	G	B♭	C#	D	E	G	F	D
G♭	Adim	G	A♭	B♭	C	D♭	E	B	C	D	E	F	F	G♭	A♭	B	D	E♭	F	A♭	G♭	E♭
G	A#dim	G#	A	B	C#	D	F	C	D♭	E♭	F	G♭	F#	G	A	C	D#	E	F#	A	G	E

CENTER PAGE

The cycle of thirds

The cycle of thirds is the basis of how chords are formed. As seen on page 6, superimposing major and minor thirds is how we create chords. You could use this cycle to find the notes of a specific chord up to the 13th degree, or to replace any chord in a progression by one of its close neighbor. We will distinguish two families. If we qualify a major third as (+) and a minor third as (-), we get:

First family

+ - + = Xmaj7

- + - = Xm7

Second family

- - + = Xm7♭5

- + + = Xmmaj7

+ + - = Xmaj7♯5

+ - - = X7

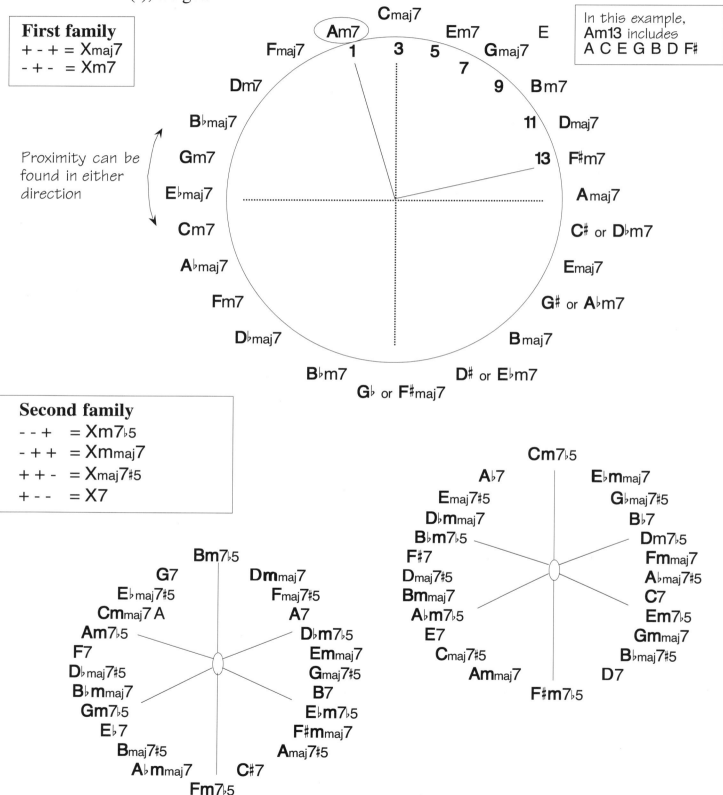

The cycle of fifths

The cycle of fifths is a crucial tool in understanding chord and key relationships that could be seen in two different ways:

1- <u>Use it to find the chords of a specific tonality</u>

Take any chord in the outer circle; its 4th is to the left and its 5th to the right.
Relative minor chords are placed just below, completing degrees I to VI of the major scale.
Only the triad built on the 7th degree of the scale escapes the group.

2- <u>Use it to find a closely related tonality for modulation</u>

The word modulation means: to change the tonality within a musical composition.

Scales are closely related when they have a difference of one or two alterations at the key signature. Neighbors in the cycle and their relative minor chords are closely related and widely used in modulation. The further chords are apart, the more unrelated they are.

The key of C has no ♯ nor ♭, the key of G has one ♯ (F♯), the key of F has one ♭ (B♭).
D (or Bm) would also be a good choice with only two alterations; F♯ and C♯ (and A♯).
B♭ is another one with alterations on B♭ and E♭.

The **outer circle** represents **major keys**; the **inner circle** represents **minor keys** of the natural minor scale (Aeolian mode). Clockwise rotation shows ascendant fifths; counter clockwise rotation shows the cycle of fourths.

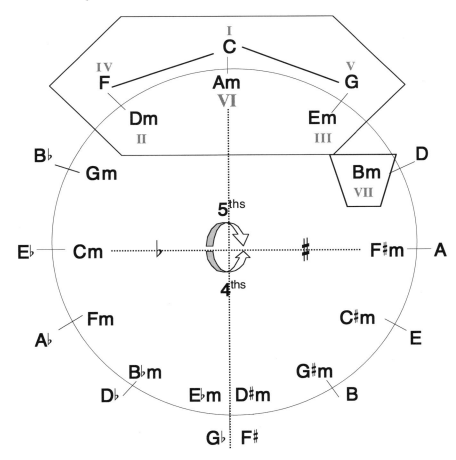

The harmonic minor scale is commonly used from classical music to heavy metal.

It can be conceived as a major scale from which the two modal notes (3 and 6) have been lowered by a half tone ($\flat$).

Scale degrees go as follow: **1, 2, $\flat$3, 4, 5, $\flat$6, 7, 8**.

The scale formula brings in a new interval of a $1^{1/2}$ tone (minor third) between the $\flat$6 and the maj7 and reads: **1 1/2 1 1 1/2 $\underline{1^{1/2}}$ 1/2**.

The types of chords created by the harmonic minor scale using the skip a note concept are mostly similar to the ones created by the major scale. They are just placed in different locations. Still, three new types appear on the 1ˢᵗ, 3ʳᵈ and 7ᵗʰ degrees of the scale.

		Chord	notes
	i	Cm^{maj}7	C E♭ G B
3	ii^ø	Dm7^{♭5}	D F A♭ C
3	III⁺	E♭^{aug}	E♭ G B D
3	iv	Fm7	F A♭ C E♭
	V	G7	G B D F
	VI	A♭maj7	A♭ C E♭ G
	vii°	Bdim7	B D F A♭

1	2	♭3	4	5	♭6	7	8
C	D	E♭	F	G	A♭	B	C
D	E♭	F	G	A♭	B	C	D
E♭	F	G	A♭	B	C	D	E♭
F	G	A♭	B	C	D	E♭	F
G	A♭	B	C	D	E♭	F	G
A♭	B	C	D	E♭	F	G	A♭
B	C	D	E♭	F	G	A♭	B

Note that III is displayed as an X_{aug} (1 3 #5) chord but could also be played as a simple major triad (1 3 5).

Here is why:

The $\flat$3ʳᵈ of the scale is located $1^{1/2}$ tones above the root. This minor third interval between root and third, makes the chord located on **III**, the relative major chord of the **I** minor chord.

Although doing so uses a note outside the scale, the **III** chord is often played as a simple major triad (M). We could always say that we are borrowing the $\flat$7ᵗʰ of the pure minor scale (Aeolian) since the 5ᵗʰ of the **III** chord is located on the 7ᵗʰ degree of the scale.

These two chords could be used in the same progression with interesting results.

Try this one out:

Cm	E♭(add9)	E♭ #5(/B)	Cm
i	**III**	**III ⁺**	**i**

The harmonic minor scale

The harmonic minor scale	See center page for more

The harmonic minor scale is sort of a solution to the weak **Vm7** of the Aeolian mode. The 3rd of the V chord falls on the 7th degree of the scale. In order to preserve the perfect cadence of $V^7 - I$, the 7th degree is played maj7 instead of ♭7 as in the Aeolian mode.

Scale formula: **1** 1/2 **1 1** 1/2 **1$^{1/2}$** 1/2   Scale degrees: **1 2 ♭3 4 5 ♭6 7 8**

Key center

i	ii^{ø}	III$^{(+)}$	iv	V	VI	vii^{o}
m	**m7$^{♭5}$**	**M, aug**	**m7**	**7**	**maj7**	**dim7**
mmaj7	dim7	maj7 (♯5)	m6$^{/9}$	7$^{♭9}$	M	♭5
mmaj$^{9/11/♭13}$		maj9 (♯5)	m7$^{♭5/9}$	7sus4	m$^{(maj7)}$	(♯5)
m♭6		add9	dim9	7$^{♯5}$, aug	6, m6	
Cm	Dm$^{♭5}$	E♭	Fm	G	A♭	B dim
C♯m	D♯m$^{♭5}$	E	F♯m	G♯	A	B♯ dim
Dm	Em$^{♭5}$	F	Gm	A	B♭	C♯ dim
E♭m	Fm$^{♭5}$	G♭	A♭m	B♭	C♭	D dim
Em	F♯m$^{♭5}$	G	Am	B	C	D♯ dim
Fm	Gm$^{♭5}$	A♭	B♭m	C	D♭	E dim
F♯m	G♯m$^{♭5}$	A	Bm	C♯	D	E♯ dim
Gm	Am$^{♭5}$	B♭	Cm	D	E♭	F♯ dim
A♭m	B♭m$^{♭5}$	C♭	D♭m	E♭	F♭	G dim
Am	Bm$^{♭5}$	C	Dm	E	F	G♯ dim
B♭m	Cm$^{♭5}$	D♭	E♭m	F	G♭	A dim
Bm	C♯m$^{♭5}$	D	Em	F♯	G	A♯ dim

- Write down two variations of the following progressions in harmonic minor mode:

Key of **A**m: **I, II, V, I**

Key of **E♭**m: **I, III, IV, VII**

-Find the key and the key center for these progressions. Write them down numerically.

/ **Em** / **F♯m7$^{♭5}$** / **B7** / **C** / **G$^{(+)}$** /

/ **Fm** / **B♭m7** / **Gm7$^{♭5}$** / **C7** /

Key	Center	Numerical
		___ ___ ___ ___ ___
		___ ___ ___ ___

The modes of the harmonic minor scale

Using modes in the minor scale is based on the same idea as in the major scale, although less common. Modes are created thinking of each note of the scale as the root of another scale.

Taking the example in **Cm**, we could create 7 different scales including the minor scale. Naming these scales is more of a challenge since there are no conventions on the subject. Here is one of the most logical way (I find): Taking the closest mode created by the major scale and specifying its altered element. They sometimes could be combined with their namesake.

Modes	Notes	Scale formula
Harmonic minor	C D E♭ F G A♭ B C	1 1/2 1 1 1/2 $1^{1/2}$ 1/2
Locrian ♮6	D E♭ F G A♭ B C D	1/2 1 1 1/2 $1^{1/2}$ 1/2 1
Ionian ♯5	E♭ F G A♭ B C D E♭	1 1 1/2 $1^{1/2}$ 1/2 1 1/2
Dorian ♯11	F G A♭ B C D E♭ F	1 1/2 $1^{1/2}$ 1/2 1 1/2 1
Phrygian major	G A♭ B C D E♭ F G	1/2 $1^{1/2}$ 1/2 1 1/2 1 1
Lydian ♯9	A♭ B C D E♭ F G A♭	$1^{1/2}$ 1/2 1 1/2 1 1 1/2
Locrian ♭♭7	B C D E♭ F G A♭ B	1/2 1 1/2 1 1 1/2 $1^{1/2}$

If you take a look at the scale formulas, you'll note that we are only moving the first interval to the end of the sequence as we go down the modes, just as we did in the major scale modes.

This obviously changes note values within the scale but the same tricks apply (page 12):

> If the two first numbers add up to **2**, **the 3rd is major**,
> if the two first numbers add up to **$1^{1/2}$**, **the 3rd is minor**.
>
> If the last number is **1/2**, **the 7th is major**,
> if the last number is **1**, **the 7th is minor**.
>
> If the two last numbers add up to **2**, **the 6th is minor**.
> if the two last numbers add up to **$1^{1/2}$**, **the 6th is major**.

▢ Most used

H.minor	1	2	♭3	4	5	♭6	7	8	2	♭3	4	5	♭6	7
Locrian ♮6		1	♭2	♭3	4	♭5	6	♭7	8					
Ionian ♯5			1	2	3	4	♯5	6	7	8				
Dorian ♯11				1	2	♭3	♯4	5	6	♭7	8			
Phrygian major					1	♭2	3	4	5	♭6	♭7	8		
Lydian ♯9						1	♯2	3	♯4	5	6	7	8	
harmonic diminished						1	♭2	♭3	♭4	♭5	♭6	♭♭7	8	

Locrian ♮6

The m7♭5 chord built on the first degree of the scale is weak and unstable. To solidify it and keep the sensation of a separate and distinct mode, avoid the key center.

Scale formula: 1/2 1 1 1/2 1$^{1/2}$ 1/2 1   Scale degrees: 1 ♭2 ♭3 4 ♭5 6 ♭7 8

						Key center
i^{ø}	**II**$^{(+)}$	**iii**	**IV**	**V**	**vi**^{o}	**vii**
m$^{7♭5}$	**M, aug**	**m7**	**7**	**maj7**	**dim7**	**m**
dim7	maj7 (#5)	m6$^{/9}$	7$^{♭9}$	M	♭5	mmaj7
m$^{no\,5}$	maj9 (#5)	m7$^{♭5/9}$	7sus4	m$^{(maj7)}$	(#5)	mmaj$^{9/11/♭13}$
	add9	dim9	7$^{#5}$, aug	6, m6		m♭6
Dm$^{♭5}$	E♭	Fm	G	A♭	B dim	Cm
D♯m$^{♭5}$	E	F♯m	G♯	A	B♯ dim	C♯m
Em$^{♭5}$	F	Gm	A	B♭	C♯ dim	Dm
Fm$^{♭5}$	G♭	A♭m	B♭	C♭	D dim	E♭m
F♯m$^{♭5}$	G	Am	B	C	D♯ dim	Em
Gm$^{♭5}$	A♭	B♭m	C	D♭	E dim	Fm
G♯m$^{♭5}$	A	Bm	C♯	D	E♯ dim	F♯m
Am$^{♭5}$	B♭	Cm	D	E♭	F♯ dim	Gm
B♭m$^{♭5}$	C♭	D♭m	E♭	F♭	G dim	A♭m
Bm$^{♭5}$	C	Dm	E	F	G♯ dim	Am
Cm$^{♭5}$	D♭	E♭m	F	G♭	A dim	B♭m
C♯m$^{♭5}$	D	Em	F♯	G	A♯ dim	Bm

- Write down two variations of the following progressions in Locrian ♮6 mode:

Key of **Gm**:   **I, IV, II, V**

Key of **Dm**: **I, III, VI, II**

-Find the key and the key center for these progressions. Write them down numerically.

/ Em$^{♭5}$ / C♯dim7 / Dm / B♭ /

/ B♭m7 / Gm7♭5 /   C7 / Fm /

Key	Center	Numerical
		___ ___ ___ ___
		___ ___ ___ ___

The dim7 chords built on degrees V and VII are only inversions of the same chord. They are interchangeable because of the minor 3rd interval separating them.

Scale formula: **1 1 1/2 1$^{1/2}$ 1/2 1 1/2**   Scale degrees: **1 2 3 4 #5 6 7 8**

					Key center	
I$^{(+)}$	ii	III	IV	v°	vi	vii^{ø}
M$^{no\ 5}$, aug	m7	7	maj7	dim7	m	m$^{7\flat5}$
maj7 (#5)	m6$^{/9}$	7$^{\flat9}$	M	$\flat$5	mmaj7	dim7
maj9 (#5)	m7$^{\flat5/9}$	7sus4	m$^{(maj7)}$	(#5)	mmaj9$^{9/11/\flat13}$	
add9	dim9	7$^{\#5}$, aug	6, m6		m$\flat$6	
E$\flat$	Fm	G	A$\flat$	B dim	Cm	Dm $^{\flat5}$
E	F#m	G#	A	B# dim	C#m	D#m $^{\flat5}$
F	Gm	A	B$\flat$	C# dim	Dm	Em $^{\flat5}$
G$\flat$	A$\flat$m	B$\flat$	C$\flat$	D dim	E$\flat$m	Fm $^{\flat5}$
G	Am	B	C	D# dim	Em	F#m $^{\flat5}$
A$\flat$	B$\flat$m	C	D$\flat$	E dim	Fm	Gm $^{\flat5}$
A	Bm	C#	D	E# dim	F#m	G#m $^{\flat5}$
B$\flat$	Cm	D	E$\flat$	F# dim	Gm	Am $^{\flat5}$
C$\flat$	D$\flat$m	E$\flat$	F$\flat$	G dim	A$\flat$m	B$\flat$m $^{\flat5}$
C	Dm	E	F	G# dim	Am	Bm $^{\flat5}$
D$\flat$	E$\flat$m	F	G$\flat$	A dim	B$\flat$m	Cm $^{\flat5}$
D	Em	F#	G	A# dim	Bm	C#m $^{\flat5}$

In the context of a namesake for the major scale, **v°** could serve as a replacement for *VIIof* VI.

Try in major scale: | **C** | **G** | **G#m7$^{\flat5}$** | **Am** | **Em** | **E** | **F** | **G#dim7** | **C** |

(I)   (V)   (*VIIof* VI)   (VI)   (III)   (III(Ionian #5))   (IV)   (V(Ionian #5))   (I)

- Write down two variations of the following progressions in Ionian #5 mode:

Key of B$\flat$: I, II, V, I

Key of E$\flat$: I, III, IV, VII

-Find the key and the key center for these progressions. Write them down numerically.

/ **F** / **F$^{\#5}$** / **Dm** / **Gm** / **B$\flat$maj7** /

/ **A** / **C#** / **D** / **E#dim** /

Key	Center		Numerical
			___ ___ ___ ___ ___

11

Dorian #11

Scale formula: **1 1/2 1$^{1/2}$ 1/2 1 1/2 1**   Scale degrees: **1 2 ♭3 #4 5 6 ♭7 8**

				Key center		
i	**II**	**III**	**iv°**	**v**	**vi⌀**	**VII**⁽⁺⁾
m7	**7**	**maj7**	dim7	**m**	**m$^{7♭5}$**	**M, aug**
m6$^{/9}$	7$^{♭9}$	M	♭5	mmaj7	dim7	maj7$^{(#5)}$
m7$^{♭5/9}$	7sus4	m$^{(maj7)}$	(#5)	mmaj$^{9/11/♭13}$		maj9 (#5)
dim9	7$^{#5}$, aug	6, m6		m♭6		add9
Fm	G	A♭	B dim	Cm	Dm $^{♭5}$	E♭
F#m	G#	A	B# dim	C#m	D#m $^{♭5}$	E
Gm	A	B♭	C# dim	Dm	Em $^{♭5}$	F
A♭m	B♭	C♭	D dim	E♭m	Fm $^{♭5}$	G♭
Am	B	C	D# dim	Em	F#m $^{♭5}$	G
B♭m	C	D♭	E dim	Fm	Gm $^{♭5}$	A♭
Bm	C#	D	E# dim	F#m	G#m $^{♭5}$	A
Cm	D	E♭	F# dim	Gm	Am $^{♭5}$	B♭
D♭m	E♭	F♭	G dim	A♭m	B♭m $^{♭5}$	C♭
Dm	E	F	G# dim	Am	Bm $^{♭5}$	C
E♭m	F	G♭	A dim	B♭m	Cm $^{♭5}$	D♭
Em	F#	G	A# dim	Bm	C#m $^{♭5}$	D

- Write down two variations of the following progressions in Dorian #11 mode:

Key of **Cm**: I, IV, V, I

Key of **Gm**: I, III, IV, VII

-Find the key and the key center for these progressions. Write them down numerically.

/ Dm / Dm7$^{/9}$ / G#dim / Fmaj7 /

/ A♭m7 / Fm7$^{♭5}$ / B♭7 / E♭m /

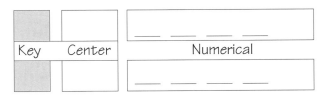

Key	Center	Numerical

Phrygian major

Scale formula: 1/2 $1^{1/2}$ 1/2 1 1/2 1 1   Scale degrees: 1 ♭2 3 4 5 ♭6 ♭7 8

			Key center			
I	**II**	**iii°**	**iv**	**v^ø**	**VI^(+)**	**vii**
7	**maj7**	dim**7**	**m**	**m**$^{7♭5}$	**M, aug**	**m7**
$7^{♭9}$	M	♭5	mmaj7	dim7	maj7(#5)	m6$^{/9}$
7sus4	m$^{(maj7)}$	(#5)	mmaj$^{9/11/♭13}$		maj9 (#5)	m7$^{♭5/9}$
$7^{#5}$, aug	6, m6		m♭6		add9	dim9
G	A♭	B dim	Cm	Dm$^{♭5}$	E♭	Fm
G#	A	B# dim	C#m	D#m$^{♭5}$	E	F#m
A	B♭	C# dim	Dm	Em$^{♭5}$	F	Gm
B♭	C♭	D dim	E♭m	Fm$^{♭5}$	G♭	A♭m
B	C	D# dim	Em	F#m$^{♭5}$	G	Am
C	D♭	E dim	Fm	Gm$^{♭5}$	A♭	B♭m
C#	D	E# dim	F#m	G#m$^{♭5}$	A	Bm
D	E♭	F# dim	Gm	Am$^{♭5}$	B♭	Cm
E♭	F♭	G dim	A♭m	B♭m$^{♭5}$	C♭	D♭m
E	F	G# dim	Am	Bm$^{♭5}$	C	Dm
F	G♭	A dim	B♭m	Cm$^{♭5}$	D♭	E♭m
F#	G	A# dim	Bm	C#m$^{♭5}$	D	Em

- Write down two variations of the following progressions in Phrygian major mode:

Key of **A**:   I, II, I, V

Key of **E♭**:   I, III, IV, V

-Find the key and the key center for these progressions. Write them down numerically.

/ **G7** / **A♭maj7** /   **G7** /   **Fm7** /

Key	Center	Numerical
		___ ___ ___ ___

/ **C7** / **D♭m6** / **A♭**^{no5} / **B♭m** /

Play these *"Spanish"* style

		___ ___ ___ ___

Lydian #9

Scale formula: **1**$^{1/2}$ **1/2 1 1/2 1 1 1/2**   Scale degrees: **1 #2 3 #4 5 6 7 8**

			Key center			
I	**ii°**	**iii**	**iv^{ø}**	**V$^{(+)}$**	**vi**	**VII**
maj7	dim**7**	**m**	**m**$^{7♭5}$	**M, aug**	**m7**	**7**
M m$^{(maj7)}$ 6, m6	♭5 (#5)	mmaj7 mmaj$^{9/11/♭13}$ m♭6	dim7	maj7(#5) maj9 (#5) add9	m6$^{/9}$ m7$^{♭5/9}$ dim9	7$^{♭9}$ 7sus4 7$^{#5}$, aug
A♭	B dim	Cm	Dm$^{♭5}$	E♭	Fm	G
A	B# dim	C#m	D#m$^{♭5}$	E	F#m	G#
B♭	C# dim	Dm	Em$^{♭5}$	F	Gm	A
C♭	D dim	E♭m	Fm$^{♭5}$	G♭	A♭m	B♭
C	D# dim	Em	F#m$^{♭5}$	G	Am	B
D♭	E dim	Fm	Gm$^{♭5}$	A♭	B♭m	C
D	E# dim	F#m	G#m$^{♭5}$	A	Bm	C#
E♭	F# dim	Gm	Am$^{♭5}$	B♭	Cm	D
F♭	G dim	A♭m	B♭m$^{♭5}$	C♭	D♭m	E♭
F	G# dim	Am	Bm$^{♭5}$	C	Dm	E
G♭	A dim	B♭m	Cm$^{♭5}$	D♭	E♭m	F
G	A# dim	Bm	C#m$^{♭5}$	D	Em	F#

- Write down two variations of the following progressions in Lydian #9 mode:

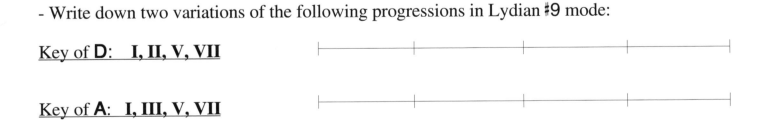

Key of **D**:   **I, II, V, VII**

Key of **A**:   **I, III, V, VII**

-Find the key and the key center for these progressions. Write them down numerically.

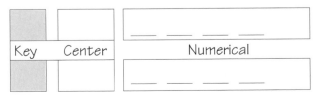

/ **F** / **G#dim** / **Cmaj7^{no5}** / **E** /

/ **E♭** / **B♭** / **D7** / **E♭** /

Key	Center	Numerical

Harmonic diminished

Scale formula: **1/2 1 1/2 1 1 1/2 1$^{1/2}$**   Scale degrees: **1 ♭2 ♭3 ♭4 ♭5 ♭6 ♭♭7 8**

	Key center					
i°	**ii**	**iiiø**	**IV$^{(+)}$**	**v**	**VI**	**VII**
dim7	m	m$^{7♭5}$	M, aug	m7	7	maj7
♭5 (♯5)	mmaj7 mmaj$^{9/11/♭13}$ m♭6	dim7	maj7(♯5) maj9 (♯5) add9	m6$^{/9}$ m7$^{♭5/9}$ dim9	7$^{♭9}$ 7sus4 7$^{♯5}$, aug	M m$^{(maj7)}$ 6, m6
B dim	**C**m	**D**m$^{♭5}$	**E♭**	**F**m	**G**	**A♭**
C dim	**D♭**m	**E♭**m$^{♭5}$	**F♭**	**G♭**m	**A♭**	**B♭♭**
C♯ dim	**D**m	**E**m$^{♭5}$	**F**	**G**m	**A**	**B♭**
D dim	**E♭**m	**F**m$^{♭5}$	**G♭**	**A♭**m	**B♭**	**C♭**
D♯ dim	**E**m	**F♯**m$^{♭5}$	**G**	**A**m	**B**	**C**
E dim	**F**m	**G**m$^{♭5}$	**A♭**	**B♭**m	**C**	**D♭**
E♯ dim	**F♯**m	**G♯**m$^{♭5}$	**A**	**B**m	**C♯**	**D**
F♯ dim	**G**m	**A**m$^{♭5}$	**B♭**	**C**m	**D**	**E♭**
G dim	**A♭**m	**B♭**m$^{♭5}$	**C♭**	**D♭**m	**E♭**	**F♭**
G♯ dim	**A**m	**B**m$^{♭5}$	**C**	**D**m	**E**	**F**
A dim	**B♭**m	**C**m$^{♭5}$	**D♭**	**E♭**m	**F**	**G♭**
A♯ dim	**B**m	**C♯**m$^{♭5}$	**D**	**E**m	**F♯**	**G**

- Write down two variations of the following progressions in harmonic diminished mode:

<u>Key of **A**:   **I, IV, V, I**</u>

<u>Key of **E♭**:   **I, III, V, VII**</u>

-Find the key and the key center for these progressions. Write them down numerically.

/ **D**dim / **F**m$^{♭5}$ / **G♭** / **E♭m** /

/ **E**dim / **A♭** / **C** / **A♭** /

Key   Center   Numerical

There is one important scale called the *melodic minor scale* we have not talked about yet. The nature of this scale is unlike any other one. It goes up and down differently. In its ascending form, we can think of it as **a major scale with a ♭3**, in its descending form, it plays as a **pure minor scale** (Aeolian: ♭7, ♭6, 5, 4, ♭3, 2, 1). The melodic minor scale is widely used in classical music.

The jazz minor scale uses the ascending melodic minor scale in both ascending and descending directions thus making it possible to think of it in a *scale-tone-chord* context. Its extensive use by jazz musicians brought its name.

Scale formula: **1   1/2   1 1 1 1   1/2**   Scale degrees: **1 2 ♭3 4 5 6 7 8**

Key center						
i	**ii**	**III⁽⁺⁾**	**IV**	**V**	**vi°**	**vii°**
m	**m7**	**maj7#5**	**7**	**7**	**m7♭5**	**m7♭5**
m^maj7	(♭9/11/13)	(9/13)	(9/#11/13)	(9/♭13)	(9/13)	(♭9/♭13)
m6		**maj7♭5**	**7♭5**	**7#5**		
Cm	Dm	E♭+	F	G	Am♭5	Bm♭5
Dm	Em	F+	G	A	Bm♭5	C#m♭5
Em	F#m	G+	A	B	C#m♭5	D#m♭5
Fm	Gm	A♭+	B♭	C	Dm♭5	Em♭5
Gm	Am	B♭+	C	D	Em♭5	F#m♭5
Am	Bm	C+	D	E	F#m♭5	G#m♭5
Bm	C#m	D+	E	F#	G#m♭5	A#m♭5

Like the major and harmonic minor scales, we could think of the Jazz minor as a mode generating scale. Here is the layout:

     Most used

Melodic m.	1	2	♭3	4	5	6	7	8	2	♭3	4	5	6	7
Dorian ♭2		1	♭2	♭3	4	5	6	♭7	8					
Lydian augmented			1	2	3	#4	#5	6	7	8				
Lydian ♭7				1	2	3	#4	5	6	♭7	8			
Hindu *See page 42*					1	2	3	4	5	♭6	♭7	8		
Locrian ♮2						1	2	♭3	4	♭5	♭6	♭7	8	
Super Locrian *(an Ionian major scale with a #1)*							1	♭2	♭3	♭4	♭5	♭6	♭7	8

Blues progressions

The dominant 12 bar Blues

The Blues comes from a mixture of culture and verbal convention between musicians. It is close to impossible to define the precise scale it originates from. This being the case, we will use the Ionian major scale to define degrees I to VII. In that context, alterations are indicated as (e.g.): ♭II or ♯V...

Considering the numerous possibilities for a dominant 7th Blues progression, only four tonalities are given for each example. They get closer to Blues Jazz as we go down the list and introduce more variations.
Bar numbers are highlighted where new concepts are introduced.

Bar	Basic dominant blues											
1	2	3	4	5	6	7	8	9	10	11	12
I	I	I	I	IV	IV	I	I	V	IV	I	V
C7	C7	C7	C7	F7	F7	C7	C7	G7	F7	C7	G7
G7	G7	G7	G7	C7	C7	G7	G7	D7	C7	G7	D7
D7	D7	D7	D7	G7	G7	D7	D7	A7	G7	D7	A7
A7	A7	A7	A7	D7	D7	A7	A7	E7	D7	A7	E7

Bar	"*Quick change*" dominant blues											
1	2	3	4	5	6	7	8	9	10	11	12
I	IV	I	I	IV	IV	I	I	V*of* V	V	I	V
E7	A7	E7	E7	A7	A7	E7	E7	F♯7	B7	E7	B7
B7	E7	B7	B7	E7	E7	B7	B7	C♯7	F♯7	B7	F♯7
F7	B♭7	F7	F7	B♭7	B♭7	F7	F7	G7	C7	F7	C7
E♭7	A♭7	E♭7	E♭7	A♭7	A♭7	E♭7	E♭7	F7	B♭7	E♭7	B♭7
C7	*F7*	*C7*	*C7*	*F7*	*F7*	*C7*	*C7*	*D7*	*G7*	*C7*	*G7*

Bar	Dominant blues #3											
1	2	3	4	5	6	7	8	9	10	11	12
I	IV	I	I	IV	IV	I	V*of* II	ii	V	I	ii - V
B♭7	E♭7	B♭7	B♭7	E♭7	E♭7	B♭7	G7	Cm7	F7	B♭7	Cm7 F7
F♯7	B7	F♯7	F♯7	B7	B7	F♯7	D♯7	G♯m7	C♯7	F♯7	G♯m7 C♯7
D♭7	G♭7	D♭7	D♭7	G♭7	G♭7	D♭7	B♭7	E♭m7	A♭7	D♭7	E♭m7 A♭7
A7	D7	A7	A7	D7	D7	A7	F♯7	Bm7	E7	A7	Bm7 E7
C7	*F7*	*C7*	*C7*	*F7*	*F7*	*C7*	*A7*	*Dm7*	*G7*	*C7*	*Dm7 G7*

Dominant blues #4

Bar	1	2	3	4	5	6	7	8	9	10	11	12
	I	IV-#iv°	I	I	IV	#iv°	I	V_{of} II	ii	V	I - V_{of} II	ii – V
	C7	F7-F#°	C7	C7	F7	F#dim	C7	A7	Dm7	G7	C7-A7	Dm7-G7
	G7	C7-C#°	G7	G7	C7	C#dim	G7	E7	Am7	D7	G7-E7	Am7-D7
	D7	G7-G#°	D7	D7	G7	G#dim	D7	B7	Em7	A7	D7-B7	Em7-A7
	A7	D7-D#°	A7	A7	D7	D#dim	A7	F#7	Bm7	E7	A7-F#7	Bm7-E7

The minor 12 bar Blues

The defining minor scale in this case is the Aeolian mode of the major scale.

Basic minor blues

Bar	1	2	3	4	5	6	7	8	9	10	11	12
	i	i	i	i	iv	iv	i	i	v	iv	i	v
	Cm7	Cm7	Cm7	Cm7	Fm7	Fm7	Cm7	Cm7	Gm7	Fm7	Cm7	Gm7
	Gm7	Gm7	Gm7	Gm7	Cm7	Cm7	Gm7	Gm7	Dm7	Cm7	Gm7	Dm7
	Dm7	Dm7	Dm7	Dm7	Gm7	Gm7	Dm7	Dm7	Am7	Gm7	Dm7	Am7
	Am7	Am7	Am7	Am7	Dm7	Dm7	Am7	Am7	Em7	Dm7	Am7	Em7

Quick-change minor blues with V^7

Bar	1	2	3	4	5	6	7	8	9	10	11	12
	i	iv	i	i	iv	iv	i	i	V	iv	i	V
	Cm7	Fm7	Cm7	Cm7	Fm7	Fm7	Cm7	Cm7	G7	Fm7	Cm7	G7
	Gm7	Cm7	Gm7	Gm7	Cm7	Cm7	Gm7	Gm7	D7	Cm7	Gm7	D7
	Dm7	Gm7	Dm7	Dm7	Gm7	Gm7	Dm7	Dm7	A7	Gm7	Dm7	A7
	Am7	Dm7	Am7	Am7	Dm7	Dm7	Am7	Am7	E7	Dm7	Am7	E7

Quick change minor blues #2

Bar	1	2	3	4	5	6	7	8	9	10	11	12
	i	iv	i	i	iv	iv	i	ii°	VI	V	i - ii°	VI - V
	Cm7	Fm7	Cm7	Cm7	Fm7	Fm7	Cm7	Ddim7	Ab7	G7	Cm7 - Ddim7	Ab7 - G7
	Gm7	Cm7	Gm7	Gm7	Cm7	Cm7	Gm7	Adim7	Eb7	D7	Gm7 - Adim7	Eb7 - D7
	Dm7	Gm7	Dm7	Dm7	Gm7	Gm7	Dm7	Edim7	Bb7	A7	Dm7 - Edim7	Bb7 - A7
	Am7	Dm7	Am7	Am7	Dm7	Dm7	Am7	Bdim7	F7	E7	Am7 - Bdim7	F7 – E7

Modern rock progressions

There are basically (and in a very large sense) two kinds of rock progressions. **One** originates directly from the dominant blues outlined in the previous pages. It uses the I, IV and V in the same pattern, still played as dominant chords. Classic examples of this can be found throughout the 60's and 70's. Just play the dominant blues progressions with a straight 4/4 beat (no shuffle) and there you go. This form is conveniently called *blues-rock*.

The other kind of rock is based on progressions similar to the ones we have seen throughout the tonal system. This type adopts the chord values prescribed by the scales they use. What makes it *Rock* can be minimized to sound, rhythm and repeated patterns. You will also find an abundant use of the sus4 chord on any major degree.

The closer we get to hard rock, the more we see that instead of extending triads to the 7th, there is a tendency to reduce them by removing the 3rd, hence creating the "**power chord**" or **X5** chord containing only 1 and 5. These chords are great for soloing and leave ample room for improvisation. They just sound "*Rock*".

The power chord is neither major nor minor by itself. It adopts (or implies) the value of the scale degree we play it on and varies according to the scale. Major and minor modes can be further defined with the addition of the 3rd in the surrounding arrangement. In the chaos of rock, punk or metal, you'll find an ample use of power chords half tone apart, regardless of the scale in use. They are sometimes used as single notes are.

The most common scales in rock/pop are:

			Not exclusively
Major	**The major scale**	1 2 3 4 5 6 7 8	Pop songs
	The Mixolydian mode	1 2 3 4 5 6 ♭7	Major rock
Minor	**The Dorian Mode**	1 2 ♭3 4 5 6 ♭7 8	Latin rock
	The Aeolian mode	1 2 ♭3 4 5 ♭6 ♭7 8	Most minor rock
	The Harmonic minor scale	1 2 ♭3 4 5 ♭6 7 8	Ballads, metal

The most common progressions in rock/pop are still the **IV – V – I** and **II – V – I**, dressed up in different ways according to the scale in use. Here are a few examples (keep your chords to a triad form or a power chord form):

I – V – I – V – I – V – I – V – IV – V – I – IV – V – I – IV – V   (Major mode)
I – IV – I – IV – VI – V – IV – I

I – IV – I – IV – VII – I – IV – I   (Mixolydian mode)
I – VII – IV – I – V – I
I – IV – I – IV – VII – IV – I – V – VI – V – I – *Vof* IV – IV – *Vof* V - V

I – V – VII - *Vof* VII – VI - *Vof* VI – V - *Vof* V – IV - *Vof* VI – II – V – I   (Aeolian mode)
I – VI – VII – III – I
I – VI – III – V – I

Song structures in the pop culture

If there is a subject with no real rules, its this one. Still, here are a number of tendencies that can be underlined.

We can define seven segments where pop-rock songs are concerned.

Segment		Tendency
Intro	IN	Serves as a prelude to the song and announces the key by either starting with the **I** chord or by creating a tension resolved with the arrival of the verse. Often adopts the progression found in the chorus played in a softer, sometimes slower way (in whole or in part).
Verse	V	This is where the singer tells his story. Typically an 8 or 16 bars sequence, divided in 4 or 8 bar patterns where the second 8 (4) bars is a repeat of the first one but ends on a different chord announcing the pre-chorus; Typically **V** in the first section and **I** in the second section.
Pre-chorus	PC	Serves as a prelude to the chorus. It could take the form of an added section or can be included as a variation within the last bars of the verse. Very often, it starts with a minor chord when the verse is major and a major chord when the verse is minor.
Chorus	CH	This is the part people remember and hum in their car. The lyrics for this segment are mostly the same throughout the song and usually contain the song title. The chorus will usually have a fuller arrangement than the verse and the vocal melody sang in a higher range. Progressions are sometimes played twice as fast. If the Verse has 1 chord per bar, the chorus may have 2…
Post-Chorus	PSC	The post-chorus is a cool down from the chorus. Most often instrumental, it is a common place for a short solo.
Bridge	B	This is the song within a song, a pause to rebuild the tension and fall back on the chorus repeated till the end. It is the location of choice for a solo but is often done with lyrics.
Ending	E	A good ending is as much a part of a song as any other segment. Some options include: Fade out the song, let the singer have the last word, slow down the 2 last bars, play a pedal on the I chord and end with a punch…

Here are a few options found in the FM radio format. Once again, no real rules here.

1 - IN — V — PC — CH — V — PC — CH — B — CH — CH — E

2 - IN — V — PC — V — PC — CH — V — PC — CH — CH — CH — FADE

3 - IN — CH — V — CH — V — PCH — CH — B — CH — CH — CH

4 - IN — V — V — CH — PSC — V — V — CH — B — CH — CH — B2 — FADE

5 - V — V — CH — V — V — CH — B — CH — CH — CH — CH

World scales chord charts

These scales have various sets of intervals, which sometimes allow both major and minor chords to be created on a given degree. 7th and $maj7^{th}$, ♭5 and #5, can also be found on a given root. Because of that, Roman numerals are all written in capitals and only notes, not triads, are displayed in the tables. An alternate notation (see page 46) is used when space is needed. As in every table before, the first set of chords, right below the Roman numerals, is taken from the skip a note concept.

To simplify things, play triads and omit the 7ᵗʰ.

You can conceive and use these scales as complete modes with interesting results or just think of them as "fake" homonym scales (page 23).

You could also use half tone related chords to bring these modes closer to the conventional tonal system. Alterations on the 5ᵗʰ can be bypassed by removing the 5ᵗʰ from the chord.

Arabian scale		1 2 3 4 ♭5 ♭6 ♭7 8			1 1 1/2 1/2 1 1 1	
I	**II**	**III**	**IV**	**V**	**VI**	**VII**
7♭5	m7♭5	7♭5sus2	m maj7	maj7#5	7#5	7
7#5	7♭5	7#5			7♭5	7♭5
C	D	E	F	G♭	A♭	B♭
D	E	F#	G	A♭	B♭	C
E	F#	G#	A	B♭	C	D
F	G	A	B♭	C♭	D♭	E♭
G	A	B	C	D♭	E♭	F
A	B	C#	D	E♭	F	G
B	C#	D#	E	F	G	A

Hindu scale		1 2 3 4 5 ♭6 ♭7 8			1 1 1/2 1 1/2 1 1	
I	**II**	**III**	**IV**	**V**	**VI**	**VII**
7	m7♭5	m7♭5	m maj7	m7	maj7#5	7
7#5, 7♭13	ø9	7♭5, 7#5	m6		maj7♭5	7♭5
C	D	E	F	G	A♭	B♭
D	E	F#	G	A	B♭	C
E	F#	G#	A	B	C	D
F	G	A	B♭	C	D♭	E♭
G	A	B	C	D	E♭	F
A	B	C#	D	E	F	G
B	C#	D#	E	F#	G	A

Neapolitan major

							1 ♭2 ♭3 4 5 6 7 8	1/2 1 1 1 1 1 1/2

I	II	III	IV	V	VI	VII
m maj7	maj7#5	7#5	7	7♭5	m7♭5	7#5
⁻6, sus4	ø, 7♭5, 7#5	7♭5	+, 7#5	7sus4 (no 5)	+, 7#5	7♭5 sus2
C	D♭	E♭	F	G	A	B
D	E♭	F	G	A	B	C#
E	F	G	A	B	C#	D#
F	G♭	A♭	B♭	C	D	E
G	A♭	B♭	C	D	E	F#
A	B♭	C	D	E	F#	G#
B	C	D	E	F#	G#	A#

Neapolitan minor

							1 ♭2 ♭3 4 5 ♭6 7 8	1/2 1 1 1 1/2 1¹ᐟ² 1/2

I	II	III	IV	V	VI	VII
m maj7	maj7	7#5	m7	7♭5	maj7	aug
sus4, ⁻Δ⁺	4, 7, Δ♭5, 7♭5	7⁺sus4, sus2	ø, 7sus2, ⁻9	7⁺, ♭9, 11, #11	Δ4, ⁻Δ, 6, ⁻6	♭5 sus2, 6 no 5
C	D♭	E♭	F	G	A♭	B
D	E♭	F	G	A	B♭	C#
E	F	G	A	B	C	D#
F	G♭	A♭	B♭	C	D♭	E
G	A♭	B♭	C	D	E♭	F#
A	B♭	C	D	E	F	G#
B	C	D	E	F#	G	A#

Enigmatic minor

							1 ♭2 ♭3 #4 5 #6 7 8	1/2 1 1¹ᐟ² 1/2 1¹ᐟ² 1/2 1/2

I	II	III	IV	V	VI	VII
m7	6 sus2,4 no 5	7	sus4	maj7#5	m#5	maj7
⁻Δ, ø, Δ°	Δsus2 no 5	6, ♭6, 7⁺	6, ⁻6	⁻Δ⁺	sus2 no 5	♭6
C	D♭	E♭	F#	G	A#	B
D	E♭	F	G#	A	B#	C#
E	F	G	A#	B	D	D#
F	G♭	A♭	B	C	D#	E
G	A♭	B♭	C#	D	F	F#
A	B♭	C	D#	E	G	G#
B	C	D	F	G♭	A	A#

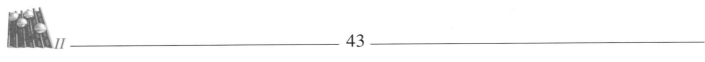

Gypsy scale		1 ♭2 3 4 5 ♭6 7 8			1/2 $1^{1/2}$ 1/2 1 1/2 $1^{1/2}$ 1/2	
I	**II**	**III**	**IV**	**V**	**VI**	**VII**
maj**7**	**7**	m^6	m maj**7**	**7**$^{♭5}$	maj**7**$^{#5}$	♭**5** sus2
aug	¯7, Δ, ¯Δ, ø	6, aug	dim$^{♭6}$	6$^{♭5}$	6$^{\text{no }5}$	#5 sus2 $^{\text{add }11}$
C	D♭	E	F	G	A♭	B
D	E♭	F#	G	A	B♭	C#
E	F	G	A	B	C	D#
F	G♭	A	B♭	C	D♭	E
G	A♭	B	C	D	E♭	F#
A	B♭	C#	D	E	F	G#
B	C	D#	E	F#	G	A#

Spanish scale		1 ♭2 3 4 5 ♭6 ♭7 8			1/2 $1^{1/2}$ 1/2 1 1/2 1 1	
I	**II**	**III**	**IV**	**V**	**VI**	**VII**
7	maj**7**	dim**7**	m maj**7**	m**7**$^{♭5}$	maj**7**$^{#5}$	m**7**
7$^{#5}$, ♭9, ♭13	6, ¯6, ♭5, Δ°	aug	Δsus4	dim7$^{♭9}$	9 sus4	ø, ¯6, sus2
C	D♭	E	F	G	A♭	B♭
D	E♭	F#	G	A	B♭	C
E	F	G#	A	B	C	D
F	G♭	A	B♭	C	D♭	E♭
G	A♭	B	C	D	E♭	F
A	B♭	C#	D	E	F	G
B	C	D#	E	F#	G	A

Oriental scale		1 ♭2 3 4 ♭5 6 ♭7 8			1/2 $1^{1/2}$ 1/2 1/2 $1^{1/2}$ 1/2 1	
I	**II**	**III**	**IV**	**V**	**VI**	**VII**
7$^{♭5}$	maj**7**$^{#5}$	♭**5**$^{\text{sus2}}$	maj**7**	**7**	m**6**	m maj**7**
6, Q(3)	dim7, aug	sus4 $^{\text{no }5}$	Δ$^{\text{sus4}}$, aug	Δ, ¯Δ, ¯7	M, aug	m♭5
C	D♭	E	F	G♭	A	B♭
D	E♭	F#	G	A♭	B	C
E	F	G#	A	B♭	C#	D
F	G♭	A	B♭	C♭	D	E♭
G	A♭	B	C	D♭	E	F
A	B♭	C#	D	E♭	F#	G
B	C	D#	E	F	G#	A

Q(3) = 1, 4, 7 and is called a quartal chord.

Hungarian major

Hungarian major		1 #2 3 #4 5 6 ♭7 8			1¹ᐟ² 1/2 1 1/2 1 1/2 1	
I	**II**	**III**	**IV**	**V**	**VI**	**VII**
7	dim**7**	m$^{♭5}$	m**7**$^{♭5}$	m$_{maj}$**7**$^{#5}$	m**7**	$_{maj}$**7**$^{#5}$ sus4
⁻7, #9, #11, ø, °	⁻6, 6, ♭9♭11	⁻Δ⁺, Δ°, Δ$^{♭5}$ 2	7$^{♭5}$, °	6$^{no 5}$	m6, ø, °7	Δ^{+sus2}
C	D#	E	F#	G	A	B♭
D	F	F#	G#	A	B	C#
E	G	G#	A#	B	C#	D#
F	G#	A	B	C	D	E
G	A#	B	C#	D	E	F#
A	C	C#	D#	E	F#	G#
B	D	D#	F	F#	G#	A#

Hungarian minor

Hungarian minor		1 2 ♭3 #4 5 ♭6 7 8			1 1/2 1¹ᐟ² 1/2 1/2 1¹ᐟ² 1/2	
I	**II**	**III**	**IV**	**V**	**VI**	**VII**
m$_{maj}$**7**	**7**$^{♭5}$	$_{maj}$**7**$^{#5}$	sus**2**$^{#5}$	$_{maj}$**7**	$_{maj}$**7**	**m6**
⁻Δ⁺, Δ°	6$^{no 5}$	⁻Δ⁺	6$_{sus2}$	Δ⁺, sus4	7, ⁻7, ⁻Δ, ø, °	6, ⁻6, ♭6, ♭9
C	D	E♭	F#	G	A♭	B
D	E	F	G#	A	B	C#
E	F#	G	A#	B	C#	D#
F	G	A♭	B	C	D	E
G	A	B♭	C#	D	E	F#
A	B	C	D#	E	F#	G#
B	C#	D	E#	F#	G#	A#

Leading whole tone

Leading whole tone		1 2 3 #4 #5 #6 7 8			1 1 1 1 1/2 1/2	
I	**II**	**III**	**IV**	**V**	**VI**	**VII**
$_{maj}$**7**$^{#5}$	**7**$^{#5}$	**7**	**7**$^{#5}$	m**7**$^{♭5}$	**7**$^{♭5}$ sus2	m$_{maj}$**7**
Δ$^{♭5}$, 7$^{♭5}$, 7$^{#5}$	7$^{♭5}$, 6$^{no 5}$	9, 7$^{♭5}$, 7⁺	7$^{♭5}$, 7^{+sus2}	7⁺, 9$^{♭5}$	7$^{#5}$	⁻6, Δ^{sus4}
C	D	E	F#	G#	A#	B
D	E	F#	G#	A#	B#	C#
E	F#	G#	A#	B#	C#	D#
F	G	A	B	C#	D	E
G	A	B	C#	D#	E	F#
A	B	C#	D#	E#	F#	G#
B	C#	D#	E#	F##	G##	A#

Chord notation

In scale degrees, 7 is played maj7 and the minor 7th is specified as ♭7. In chord notation, 7 is played as ♭7 and the major 7th is specified as maj7. To preserve this convention, the maj7 is indicated as #7 in the chord formulas.

MAJOR MODE				MINOR MODE	
BASIC CHORDS					
			Alternate notation		
X	= 1 3 5	M		Xm	= 1 ♭3 5
X7	= 1 3 5 7		X⁻7	Xm7	= 1 ♭3 5 7
Xmaj7	= 1 3 5 #7	X△	X⁻△	Xmmaj7	= 1 ♭3 5 #7
X7sus4	= 1 4 5 7	X7⁴	X⁻6	Xm6	= 1 ♭3 5 6
X6	= 1 3 5 6				
Xsus4	= 1 4 5	X4			
X7/6	= 1 3 5 6 7				
Q(3)	= 1 4 7	Q(3)		Can replace a 7sus4 chord	
ALTERED BASIC CHORDS					
Xmaj7#5	= 1 3 #5 #7	X△+			
X7#5	= 1 3 #5 7	X7⁺			
X7♭5	= 1 3 ♭5 7		X⌀	Xm7♭5	= 1 ♭3 ♭5 7
X♭5	= 1 3 ♭5		X°	Xdim	= 1 ♭3 ♭5
Xaug	= 1 3 #5	X⁺	X°7	Xdim7	= 1 ♭3 ♭5 ♭7
COMPOSED CHORDS					
X9	= 1 3 5 7 9		X⁻9	Xm9	= 1 ♭3 5 7 9
Xmaj9	= 1 3 5 #7 9	X9△	X⁻9△	Xm9maj7	= 1 ♭3 5 #7 9
X6/9	= 1 3 5 6 9		X⁻6/9	Xm6/9	= 1 ♭3 5 6 9
X11	= 1 3 5 7 9 11		X⁻11	Xm11	= 1 ♭3 5 7 9 11
X13	= 1 3 5 7 9 11 13		X⁻13	Xm13	= 1 ♭3 5 7 9 11 13
Xadd 9	= 1 3 5 9				
Xadd 11	= 1 3 5 11				
Xadd 13	= 1 3 5 13				
Xmaj #11	= 1 3 5 #7 9 #11	X△#11			
Xmaj 13	= 1 3 5 #7 9 11 13	X△13			
ALTERED COMPOSED CHORDS					
				No minor equivalent	
X7♭9	= 1 3 5 7 ♭9				
X7#9	= 1 3 5 7 #9			In alternate notation:	
X9♭5	= 1 3 ♭5 7 9			- = minor	
X9#5	= 1 3 #5 7 9	X⁺9		+ = #5	
X9#11	= 1 3 5 7 9 #11			△ = maj7	
X13♭9	= 1 3 5 7 ♭9 11 13			⌀ = m7♭5	
X13♭9♭5	= 1 3 ♭5 7 ♭9 11 13			O = dim	

Keyboard diagram showing scale degrees:

Black keys (upper labels): ♭2 / #2 (between 1,2), ♭3 / #2, ♭5 / #4, ♭6 / #5, ♭♭7, 7, ♭9, #9, #11, ♭13

White keys (lower labels): 1, 2, 3, 4, 5, 6, #7, 8, 9, 10, 11, 12, 13

Quiz answers

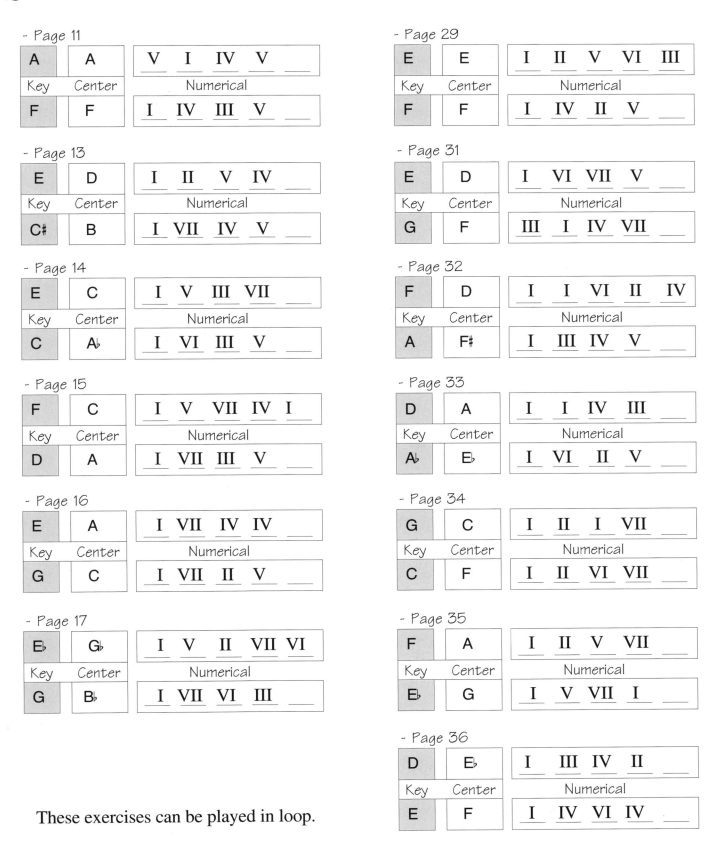

- Page 11

A	A	V	I	IV	V		
Key	Center			Numerical			
F	F	I	IV	III	V		

- Page 13

E	D	I	II	V	IV		
Key	Center			Numerical			
C#	B	I	VII	IV	V		

- Page 14

E	C	I	V	III	VII		
Key	Center			Numerical			
C	A♭	I	VI	III	V		

- Page 15

F	C	I	V	VII	IV	I
Key	Center			Numerical		
D	A	I	VII	III	V	

- Page 16

E	A	I	VII	IV	IV	
Key	Center			Numerical		
G	C	I	VII	II	V	

- Page 17

E♭	G♭	I	V	II	VII	VI
Key	Center			Numerical		
G	B♭	I	VII	VI	III	

- Page 29

E	E	I	II	V	VI	III
Key	Center			Numerical		
F	F	I	IV	II	V	

- Page 31

E	D	I	VI	VII	V	
Key	Center			Numerical		
G	F	III	I	IV	VII	

- Page 32

F	D	I	I	VI	II	IV
Key	Center			Numerical		
A	F#	I	III	IV	V	

- Page 33

D	A	I	I	IV	III	
Key	Center			Numerical		
A♭	E♭	I	VI	II	V	

- Page 34

G	C	I	II	I	VII	
Key	Center			Numerical		
C	F	I	II	VI	VII	

- Page 35

F	A	I	II	V	VII	
Key	Center			Numerical		
E♭	G	I	V	VII	I	

- Page 36

D	E♭	I	III	IV	II	
Key	Center			Numerical		
E	F	I	IV	VI	IV	

These exercises can be played in loop.

Conclusion

This is it; we've now come to the end of the book. Did we cover every aspect of music harmony? Absolutely not! The ramifications of music are so large and complex, the styles so numerous; we could get lost in the possibilities created by only twelve notes. One important area of harmony that has not been touched here is *voice leading*. You may want to read more on this one.

I hope this volume will keep on being useful to you as a reference and as a source of inspiration for many years to come. Detach the extra center page carefully and stick it on the wall so you always have it in front of you (I did). It makes working with modes easy.

This book is based on the *how*, not the *why*. Theory is great but can sometimes hinder creativity. As you can see, there are no real rules, only some conventions that will make your compositions accessible to a broad audience. If you feel there are some missing links and wish to further your comprehension of the tonal system, here are a few books I would suggest:

Harmony Book One ——————— A must
Mark Sarnecki   for basis in voice
Frederick Harris Music   leading and more.

The New Harmony Book ————— A clear and
Frank Haunschild   extensive view of
AMA Verlag   modern harmony

Théorie de la musique ————— Symbols and notation.
Henry Lemoine   A must for a clear unders-
or an English theory book equivalent   tanding of the tonal system.

The Guitar Grimoire ————— A what's where on guitar.
Scales and modes   Easy to use, well done.
Adam Kadmon
Carl Fisher LLC

THE ART OF CHORDS ————— Understanding chord
Created for guitarists   positions in a logical way.
Stéphane Gagnon
Carl Fischer LLC worldwide
Canadian Print Music exclusively in Canada

Have fun and keep on playing!

Your own progressions

Your own progressions

II